The Heinemann Science Scheme

Foundation Edition

Byron Dawson

Heinemann Educational Publishers
Halley Court, Jordan Hill, Oxford, OX2 8EJ
Part of Harcourt Education Limited

Heinemann is the registered trademark of
Harcourt Education Limited

© Harcourt Education Limited 2003

First published 2003

07 06 05 04
10 9 8 7 6 5 4 3 2

British Library Cataloguing in Publication Data is available from the British Library on request.

ISBN 0 435 58332 8

Copyright notice
All rights reserved. No part of this publication may be reproduced in any form or by any means (including photocopying or storing it in any medium by electronic means and whether or not transiently or incidentally to some other use of this publication) without the written permission of the copyright owner, except in accordance with the provisions of the Copyright, Designs and Patents Act 1988 or under the terms of a licence issued by the Copyright Licensing Agency Ltd, 90 Tottenham Court Road, London W1T 4LP. Applications for the copyright owner's written permission should be addressed to the publisher.

Edited by Ruth Holmes

Typeset by Techset Ltd, Gateshead

Original illustrations © Harcourt Education Limited 2003

Illustrated by Hardlines

Printed and bound in Italy by Printer Trento S.r.l.

Cover photo: © Science Photo Library

Picture research by Bea Thomas

Index by Ann Hall

Acknowledgements
Every effort has been made to contact copyright holders of material reproduced in this book. Any omissions will be rectified in subsequent printings if notice is given to the publishers.

The author and publishers would like to thank the following for permission to use photographs:

T = top **B** = bottom **R** = right **L** = left **M** = middle

SPL = Science Photo Library

2 T Corbis/Tempsport, **M** Ecoscene; **5 T and TM** SPL, **BM** KPT Photos; **B** Alamy; **6 TL** Ecoscene/Kjell Sandved, **TR** Ecoscene/Sally Morgan, **ML** Ecoscene/Alan Towse, **MR** Papillo/Mikael Svensson, **B** Ecoscene/Stephen Coyne; **7 TL** Bruce Coleman, **ML** Ecoscene/Justine Pickett, **TR** Ecoscene/Derrick Beacos; **8 T** Peter Morris; **9 TR** SPL, **MR** SPL; **10 TR** Ecoscene, **MR** Corbis/Ed Young; **11 TR, TM, TL all** Peter Morris; **12 TR** Photodisc, **MR** Corbis/Joseph Sohn; **13** Corbis; **14** Corbis/Duomo; **15 BL, BR all** SPL; **16 TR** Peter Morris, **MR** SPL, **ML** Corbis/Lawrence Manning; **17** Photodisc; **19 BR** SPL; **20 L and R** SPL; **21** Gareth Boden; **23 B** Ecoscene/Andrew Brown; **24 B** Gareth Boden; **25 TR** Garden Matters, **MR** SPL; **26 BM, BR all** Gareth Boden; **29** Ecoscene; **30** Ecoscene/Anthony Harrison; **31 TR** Peter Morris, **MR** Gareth Boden; **32 TR** Peter Morris, **BR** Environmental Images; **34** SPL; **35** SPL; **36 TL** Ecoscene/Robin Redfern, **TLM** Ecoscene/Chinch Gryniewicz, **TRM** Ecoscene/Robin Williams, **TR** Ecoscene/Robert Pickett; **38** Ecoscene/Michael Howes; **39** Environmental Images/Toby Adamson; **40 TL, TM and TR all** Gareth Boden; **41 M** Alamy, **BL** Corbis/Felix Zaska, **BR** Ecoscene/John Farmar; **42 T and M both** Gareth Boden, **B** Andrew Lambert; **43** Corbis/Frank Lane; **44 T** SPL. **M** Gareth Boden; **46** Gareth Boden; **47 TR** Gareth Boden, **BL** Peter Morris; **48** Gareth Boden; **49 BR** Peter Morris, **BL** Corbis/Kit Houghton; **52 TM** Corbis/Kevin Morris, **TR** Corbis/Araldo de Lucia, **BL and BM both** Gareth Boden; **53 T** SPL; **54 both** Gareth Boden; **55** Gareth Boden; **56 TR** Gareth Boden, **MR** Andrew Lambert, **BL, BLM, BRM and BR all** Gareth Boden; **58 both** Gareth Boden; **59 all** Gareth Boden; **60 T** Corbis/Arne Hodalic, **M** Corbis/James Amos; **61 TR** Gareth Boden, **ML** Capital Pictures; **62 TL and TM** Corbis/Michael Brusselle, **TR** Ecoscene/Frank Blackburn, **B** Holt Studios; **63 B** Ecoscene/Peter Hulme; **64 T** Environmental Images, **ML** Corbis/Michael Nicholson, **MR** Corbis/Roger Wood, **B** Ecoscene/Andrew Brown; **66 both** Gareth Boden; **68 TL and TR** Gareth Boden, **ML and MR** Gareth Boden, **B** Ecoscene/David Pearson; **69 T** Ecoscene/Nick Hawkes, **B** SPL; **70 M** Corbis, **B** Corbis/Gunter Marx; **72 T** Corbis/Stephanie Maze, **B** Byron Dawson; **73** SPL/Cordelia Molloy; **74 TL** Ecoscene, **TR** Peter Morris, **ML** Corbis/Paul Souders, **MR** Peter Morris, **BL** Environmental Images/Sam Cranston, **BR** Gareth Boden; **75** SPL; **76 T** Peter Morris, **M and B** Corbis; **77** Ecoscene/Andy Hibbert; **78 and 80 both** Gareth Boden; **82 T** Peter Morris, **M** Peter Gould, **BL** Colorsport, **BR** Photodisc; **83 TL and TR** Alamy, **TM** Andrew Lambert; **85** Environmental Images/Leslie Garland; **91** Photodisc; **93** Peter Gould; **94** Andrew Lambert; **96** Photodisc; **98 both** Corbis; **100** Photodisc; **103 T** SPL, **B** Gareth Boden; **104 T** Corbis/Ales Feuzer, **M** Gareth Boden, **B** Corbis; **106** Photodisc; **108 T** Corbis/Paul Saunders, **B** Ecoscene/Philip Colla; **109 T** Alamy, **B** SPL; **110 T** Photodisc, **B** Corbis/Kevin Morris; **111** SPL; **113** Corbis/Robert Holmes; **116** Nick Sample; **117** Robert Harding; **119** Peter Morris; **120** Ecoscene/Wayne Lawler; **121** Robert Harding

Tel: 01865 888058 www.heinemann.co.uk

Introduction

Welcome to Heinemann Science Scheme!

This is the third Foundation book in a series of three. They cover all the science you need to learn at Key Stage 3.

The book is divided into twelve units. Each unit has several topics. A topic is on two pages. In each topic you will find:

- **Questions as you go along like this:**

  b What is the solute in salt solution?

  These are quick questions to check that you understand things before you carry on.

- **Questions in a box at the end of the spread with this heading:**

  QUESTIONS

  These help you bring together everything in the topic.

- **A list of key points at the end with this heading:**

  KEY POINTS

  These summarise what you have studied in the topic.

Important words are highlighted in **bold**. They are all in a glossary at the back of the book with their meanings. You can look them up as you work through the book.

As you study Heinemann Science Scheme your teacher will give you activities and extra questions from the teacher's pack. There are also tests to help you and your teachers keep track of how you're doing.

We hope you enjoy studying science with Heinemann Science Scheme.

Contents

Introduction — iii
Contents — iv, v

A Inheritance and selection

- A1 What causes variation: inheritance — 2
- A2 What causes variation: environment — 4
- A3 Selective breeding in animals — 6
- A4 Selective breeding in plants — 8
- A5 What is a clone? — 10

B Fit and healthy

- B1 What do we mean by fit? — 12
- B2 The breathing system and smoking — 14
- B3 Drugs and alcohol — 16
- B4 Movement and exercise — 18

C Plants and photosynthesis

- C1 How do plants grow? — 20
- C2 What is the role of the leaf in photosynthesis? — 22
- C3 What happens to glucose produced in the leaves? — 24
- C4 What is the role of the root in photosynthesis? — 26
- C5 Why are green plants important in the environment? — 28

D Plants for food

- D1 Where does our food come from? — 30
- D2 How do fertilisers affect plant growth? — 32
- D3 How does competition affect plant growth? — 34
- D4 How do pests affect plant growth? — 36
- D5 What is the perfect environment for growing plants? — 38

E Reactions of metals and metal compounds

- E1 Why are metals useful? — 40
- E2 How do metals react with acids? — 42
- E3 How do carbonates react with acids? — 44
- E4 How do oxides react with acids? — 46
- E5 How do alkalis react with acids? — 48
- E6 Balanced equations — 50

F Patterns of reactivity

- F1 What makes metals change? — 52
- F2 How do metals react with water? — 54
- F3 Do all metals react with acids? — 56
- F4 Can metals displace each other? — 58
- F5 How is reactivity useful? — 60

G Environmental chemistry

G1	How are soils different?	62
G2	How do rocks change?	64
G3	What causes acid rain?	66
G4	What does acid rain do?	68
G5	What's happening to the environment?	70

H Using chemistry

H1	What happens when fuels burn?	72
H2	Do other chemical reactions supply energy?	74
H3	What new materials can we make from chemicals?	76
H4	What happens to atoms in a chemical reaction?	78
H5	Proving the theory of conservation of mass	80

I Energy and electricity

I1	How is energy useful for doing things?	82
I2	How does electricity transfer energy?	84
I3	Models of electricity	86
I4	How do we use electricity?	88
I5	Where do we get electricity from?	90
I6	Why is energy wasted?	92

J Gravity and space

J1	What is gravity?	94
J2	How does gravity change?	96
J3	Models of the Solar System	98
J4	Satellites	100

K Speeding up

K1	How fast is it moving?	102
K2	Getting faster	104
K3	How do forces affect speed?	106
K4	How can we increase speed?	108
K5	How do parachutes work?	110

L Pressure and moments

L1	What is pressure?	112
L2	What is hydraulics?	114
L3	What is pneumatics?	116
L4	How do levers work?	118
L5	Using counterweights	120
L6	Moments	122

Glossary   124

Index   129

A Inheritance and selection

A1 WHAT CAUSES VARIATION: INHERITANCE

What characteristics can be inherited?

Look at the picture of the Brazilian football team. They all look different. This is because they have different characteristics.

All living things **inherit** characteristics from their parents.

ⓐ Look at the picture of the calf. Give two characteristics that the calf has inherited from its mother.

How are characteristics inherited?

You inherit characteristics from both your mother and your father. This is because you were made when a sperm from your father fertilised an egg from your mother.

Look at the picture of the family.

ⓑ Did the girl inherit her dark hair from her mother or father?

ⓒ Did the boy inherit his thin eyebrows from his mother or father?

How is the information passed from parent to child?

The father makes sperm cells. The mother makes egg cells. Both these cells have a nucleus which carries information from the parents. The information is carried by **genes**.

d What carries the information from the mother and the father?

The sperm cell fertilises the egg cell. The genes in each nucleus are mixed together.

You inherit some things from your mother and some things from your father. It all depends which of their genes you get. You might get the gene for blue eyes from your mother and the gene for blond hair from your father.

Because this variation is inherited, it is called **inherited variation**.

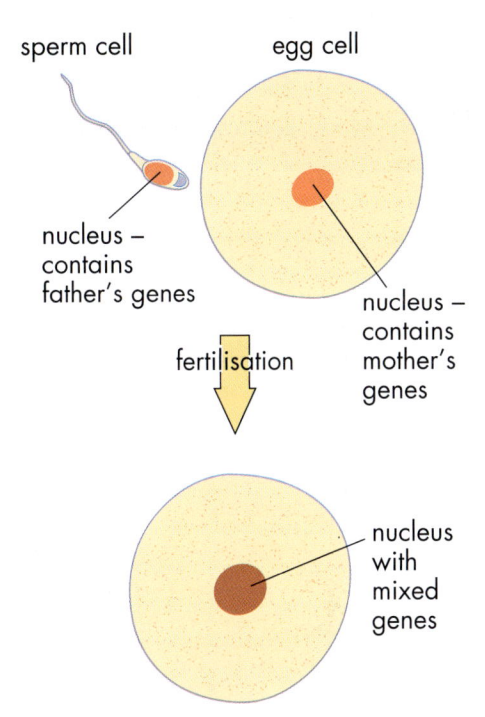

Why are children from the same parents not identical?

Look at the family tree again on the opposite page. The two children are very different even though they have the same parents.

This is because they inherited different genes from each parent. It's like playing cards. You never deal the same hand twice.

QUESTIONS

Copy these sentences and fill in the spaces using the words below:

different   genes   inherit   variation

All living things _____ information from their parents. The information is carried in the _____. Everyone inherits a _____ set of genes. This is why we are all different. The differences are called _____.

KEY POINTS

- You inherit characteristics from your parents.
- The information is carried in genes.
- We all look different because we all inherit different genes.

Inheritance and selection

A2 WHAT CAUSES VARIATION: ENVIRONMENT

Why do identical twins look the same?

If everyone is born with a different set of genes, why do identical twins look the same? The answer is because they have inherited the same set of genes. Because their genes are the same, the twins look the same.

Look at the picture. It shows an egg cell after fertilisation. It normally passes down to the uterus where it develops into a new baby.

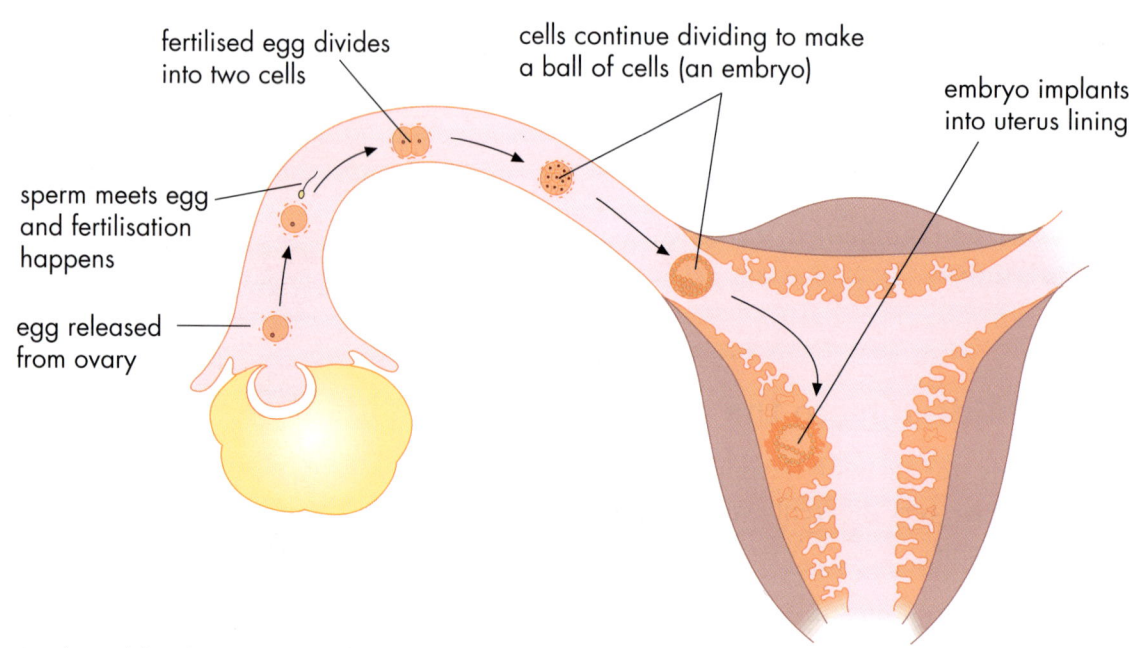

- fertilised egg divides into two cells
- cells continue dividing to make a ball of cells (an embryo)
- embryo implants into uterus lining
- sperm meets egg and fertilisation happens
- egg released from ovary

Look at this picture. Something strange has happened. The embryo has split in two after fertilisation. Each half contains exactly the same genes. Each half will grow into a new baby. They will be identical twins.

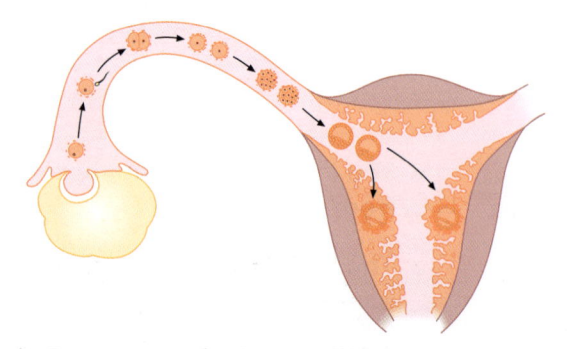

a If identical twins have the same genes, can they be different sexes?

Inheritance and selection

What is environmental variation?

Identical twins look the same when they are born, but they soon begin to look different.
These 'identical twin' babies look the same.

The 'identical twin' girls below look slightly different.

This is called **environmental variation**. It is caused by things that happen to us in our surroundings. The girls in the picture have had their hair cut differently. This is an example of environmental variation.

How do inherited variation and environmental variation affect us?

We all look the way we do because of both genes and the environment. We inherit our genes and then the environment changes our characteristics.

Imagine you inherited genes to make you tall, white skinned and intelligent. The environment will affect each of these features.

- If you don't get enough food from birth, you will not grow to be tall.
- If you spend a lot of time in the sun your skin will tan and turn browner.
- If you don't go to school and study you will not be as intelligent.

Look at the photos of two different kinds of tomato.

The big beefsteak tomato has inherited genes to make it large.

The small cherry tomatoes have inherited genes to make them small.

But not all the cherry tomatoes are the same. They are all slightly different. This difference is caused by the environment.

QUESTIONS

Look at the following types of variation. Copy them and write **inherited** or **environmental** next to each one.

scar on leg   eye colour
hair length   shape of ear

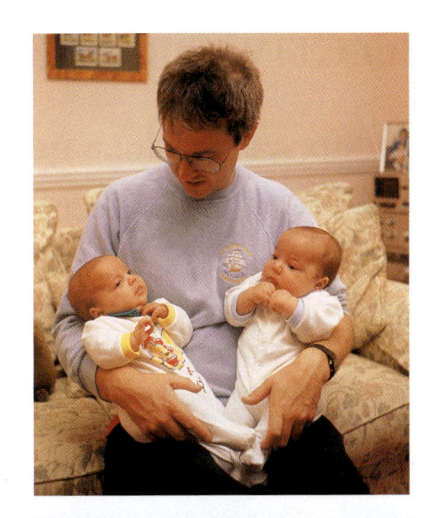

KEY POINTS

- Identical twins have the same genes.
- Variation can also be caused by the environment.

Inheritance and selection

A3 SELECTIVE BREEDING IN ANIMALS

How do we produce new breeds of animal?

Look at the pictures of dogs. They all look different. They are all different breeds.

a Write down one characteristic for each breed that is different from the others.

Some breeders take their dogs to dog shows. Look at the picture opposite. These dogs are big with long hair.

The dogs look like this because of **selective breeding**. The breeders selected parents with the characteristics that they wanted the puppies to have. They selected parents that were big and had long hair. They bred these selected parents together. Then the genes for being big and having long hair would be passed on to their puppies.

b Imagine you wanted to breed a dog with lots of spots. How would you choose the parent dogs to breed from?

Farmers also use selective breeding

Modern farm animals are the result of selective breeding over hundreds of years.

- Dairy cows have been bred to produce lots of milk.

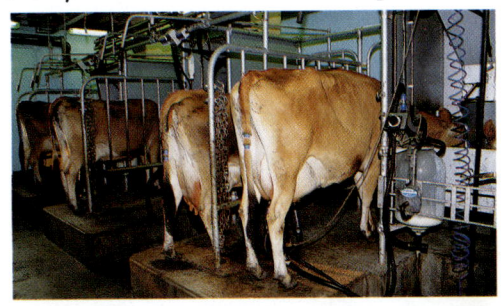

- Sheep have been bred to produce lots of wool.

- Meat cattle have been bred to produce lots of meat.

c What characteristics do farmers breed sheep and cows for?

Why are some breeds conserved?

In selective breeding people choose the genes that they want in their plants and animals. If we are not careful we might lose the genes that we do not choose.

These genes might turn out to be very useful in the future. They might protect the animal from disease or help it survive when there is not much water. At rare breed centres people collect animals that have these genes. By breeding them they make sure that the genes are not lost for future generations.

QUESTIONS

Copy these sentences choosing only the correct words:

Selective breeding is used by farmers to produce cows that give **more** / **less** milk. At rare breed centres genes are kept for **future** / **past** generations.

KEY POINTS

- In selective breeding people select the characteristics that they want in animals and plants.

A4 SELECTIVE BREEDING IN PLANTS

Why do plant breeders use selective breeding?

In the supermarket you see lots of different fruits and vegetables. Many have been produced by selective breeding. They are bred to look good and taste nice.

Look at the picture. It shows different types of lettuce.

Here are some other reasons for selectively breeding plants:

- To make them more resistant to cold weather. The farmer will be able to grow the crop for longer and make more money.

- To make them more resistant to rotting. The farmer will lose less crop and make more money.

a List three characteristics a farmer might breed fruit and vegetables for.

How does fertilisation happen in plants?

Fertilisation happens inside flowers. The female egg cells are inside the ovary. The male pollen cells are inside pollen grains.

The pollen grains travel from one flower to another. They are either blown by the wind or carried by insects.

The pollen grain lands on the stigma of the new flower. It grows a tube down towards the ovary. The male pollen cell goes down the tube to fertilise the female egg cell.

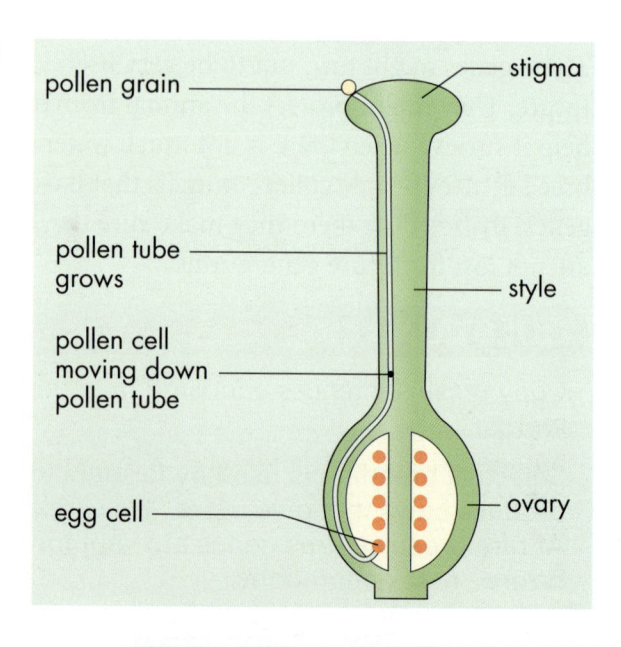

Look at the picture. You can see the pollen grain growing a pollen tube.

Once the egg cell has been fertilised, it divides and grows into a seed. This seed will later grow into a new plant.

How do plant breeders do selective breeding?

Selective breeding in plants is just like selective breeding in animals.

First you choose the parent plants with the characteristics that you want. Then you fertilise the egg cell from one parent using a pollen grain from another parent.

A plant breeder uses a fine brush to collect pollen from one flower. The brush then transfers the pollen to the other flower.

b How does the breeder transfer pollen from one flower to another?

It sounds very easy. But there can be problems.

- Pollen from other flowers may reach the stigma first. Breeders often put paper bags over the flowers to stop this happening.
- The pollen grains and egg cells may be ready at different times. Breeders often store pollen to use later.
- It takes a long time to see if you have been successful. It will be another year before the seed grows and you can see what the new plant looks like.

c Why is selective breeding in plants quite difficult?

QUESTIONS

Copy these sentences and fill in the spaces using the words below:

grain   egg   resistance   seed

Fruit and vegetables are not only bred for taste but also characteristics such as _____ to rotting. To breed plants a pollen _____ fertilises an _____ cell. This then grows into a _____.

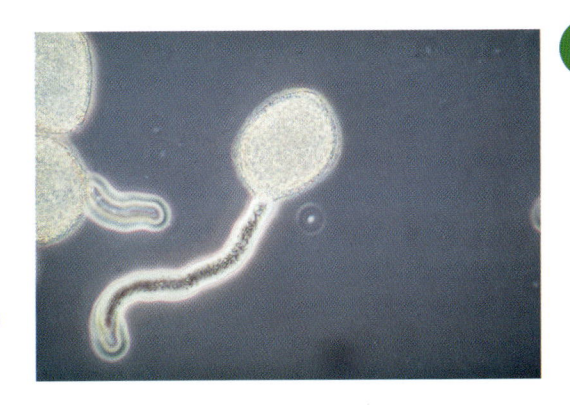

KEY POINTS

- People do selective breeding in plants as well as animals.

Inheritance and selection

A5 WHAT IS A CLONE?

What is asexual reproduction?

Most plants reproduce with pollen cells and egg cells. This is called **sexual reproduction**.

But some plants can use **asexual reproduction**. They simply grow a new baby plant.

Look at the spider plant. It has grown a baby plant which is almost ready to separate. Because it has been made from only one parent plant, its genes are identical to its parent's genes. We call it a **clone** of the parent.

a Why is the baby spider plant called a clone?

How are clones produced?

After years of selective breeding, a plant breeder may have just the kind of plant that they want. It would be useful to make clones of this plant. This would give lots of copies to grow and sell.

Just like spider plants, strawberry plants make their own clones.

Look at the picture below. You can see how the parent plant makes lots of baby clones.

How can breeders make clones?

Some plants do not make clones for themselves. If a breeder wants a clone, then they will have to make one.

First take a side shoot or piece of stem from the parent plant. This is called a cutting.

Dip the cutting in rooting powder.

Plant the cutting.

Soon you will have a healthy growing clone.

b What is a cutting?

Why are some people worried about cloning?

- Because all clones are identical, a disease that kills one of them would kill all of them.
- Some people believe it is not natural and against God. They are worried that someone will try to clone a human being.

QUESTIONS

Copy these sentences and fill in the spaces using the words below:

   cuttings   asexual   clone

Clones are produced by _____ reproduction. Strawberry runners are an example of a _____. Plant breeders can make clones by taking _____.

KEY POINTS

- Cloning happens in nature.
- Plant breeders use cloning to make more plants the same as the parent.

Inheritance and selection

B Fit and healthy

B1 WHAT DO WE MEAN BY FIT?

What is fitness?

Fitness is a measure of how well our heart and lungs work. Some people follow a fitness programme to get fit. This tells them what exercises to do, what to eat, and how to cut down on alcohol and cigarettes.

You can measure fitness in different ways. You can:

1. find out your heart rate when you are resting
2. do 30 seconds of exercise and find out how long it takes your heart to return to normal afterwards
3. press against some bathroom scales and see how hard you can push.

a How can we measure fitness?

How do we release energy from food?

All the cells in your body need energy. They get this energy from **respiration**. In respiration, glucose and oxygen react to form carbon dioxide and water. Energy is also released for the cells to use.

Look at the word equation. It shows what happens during respiration.

$$\text{glucose} + \text{oxygen} \xrightarrow{\text{energy is released}} \text{carbon dioxide} + \text{water}$$

All your cells need to respire. For this to happen you need:

- a **digestive system**. Glucose from food is absorbed into your blood here.
- a **breathing system**. Oxygen from the air is absorbed into your blood in the lungs.
- a **circulatory system**. Blood carries the glucose and oxygen to all the cells of your body.

These people are fit. They have just finished a marathon.

Why is diet important?

It is not just glucose that you need from your food. Your body needs a **balanced diet** to give you all of the nutrients that you need.

ⓑ Why do you need a balanced diet?

These are some of the nutrients that your body needs.

Nutrient	Job in your body
carbohydrates such as glucose	for energy
fat	for energy and warmth
protein	for growth and repair
vitamins	keeps you healthy
minerals	keeps you healthy
fibre	keeps your digestive system working properly
water	helps chemical reactions happen

It is important to eat the right amount of each nutrient. If you eat too much fat it can block blood vessels. If you eat too little fat and carbohydrate you starve.

The picture shows a little boy who has not eaten enough food. When someone does not eat enough of a particular nutrient it is called a **deficiency**.

ⓒ What is a deficiency?

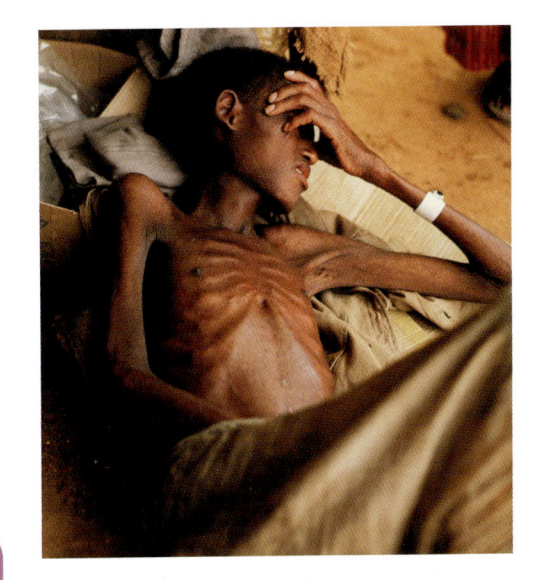

QUESTIONS

Copy these sentences and write **true** or **false** next to each one:

We get energy from our food by the process of respiration.

A balanced diet only contains some of the nutrients that we need.

KEY POINTS

- We get energy from glucose and oxygen by respiration.
- A balanced diet contains all the nutrients that we need.

B2 THE BREATHING SYSTEM AND SMOKING

How do you breathe?

For your body cells to respire they need to use oxygen and get rid of carbon dioxide. When you breathe you take oxygen into your blood from the air. You also get rid of carbon dioxide from your blood into the air.

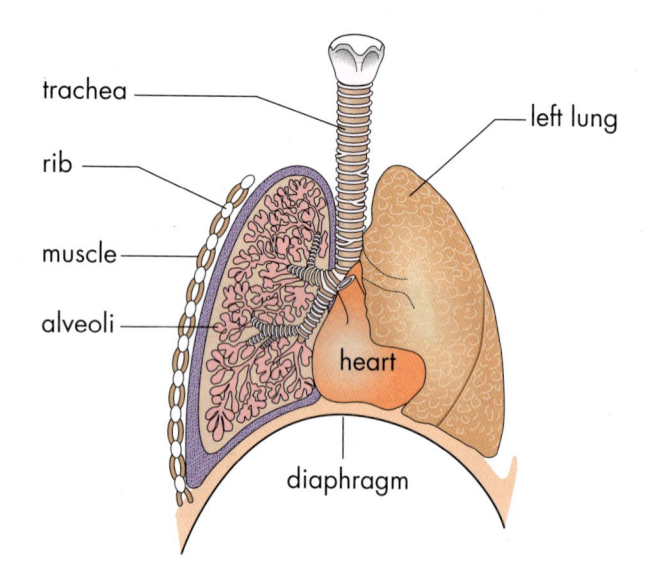

How do you breathe in?

When you breathe in, your rib cage moves up and out. The diaphragm muscle at the bottom of the lungs flattens down. This increases the space inside your chest and air rushes into the lungs.

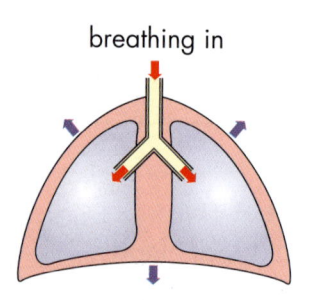

a How do you breathe in?

How do you breathe out?

When you breathe out, your rib cage moves down and in. The diaphragm domes up. This squashes the lungs and air rushes out.

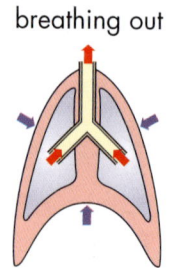

b How do you breathe out?

How much do you breathe?

Look at the picture.

The sprinter needs lots of energy to run fast. She needs extra oxygen. So she breathes more quickly and deeply.

People who do a lot of exercise can breathe more deeply than people who do little exercise.

How does cigarette smoke affect your lungs?

B2

Cigarette smoke contains lots of harmful chemicals. Many of the chemicals reduce the amount of oxygen that gets to your body cells.

This means the cells cannot release enough energy. Because of this smokers often feel tired and out of breath.

When a pregnant mother smokes, her baby will get less oxygen. This can be very harmful to the baby.

c Why should pregnant mothers not smoke?

Tar is one harmful substance in cigarette smoke. Tar is a mixture of chemicals. It causes lung cancer.

Your windpipe is lined with small hairs that keep it clean. Tar damages these hairs so that dirt and bacteria build up. This is why smokers cough a lot and have chest infections such as bronchitis.

This is the lung of a healthy person.

This is the lung of a smoker. You can see the black tar that has built up in it.

d Name a poisonous substance found in cigarette smoke.

QUESTIONS

Copy these sentences and fill in the spaces using the words below:

cancer   down   ribs

When you breathe in your _____ move up and out and your diaphragm flattens _____. Cigarette smoke contains tar that causes _____.

KEY POINTS

- Your lungs take in oxygen from the air and get rid of carbon dioxide.
- Cigarette smoke contains chemicals that damage your lungs.

Fit and healthy

B3 DRUGS AND ALCOHOL

What is a drug?

A **drug** is a chemical that affects the way your body works.

There are three main groups of drugs.

- **Medical drugs**. Medical drugs are to make you feel better when you are ill.
- **Recreational drugs**. These include alcohol, nicotine and caffeine. Alcohol makes you feel happy and relaxed. Nicotine and caffeine make you more alert.
- **Illegal drugs**. These include cannabis, amphetamines, ecstasy and heroin. The table below tells you more about these drugs.

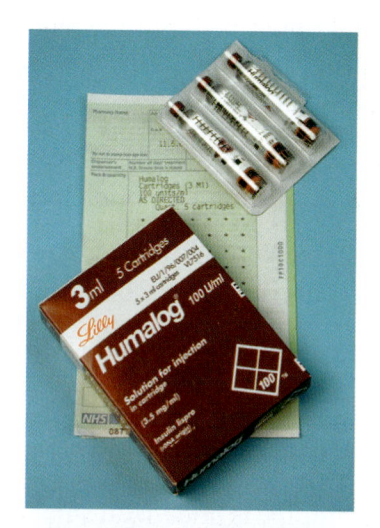

a Name four illegal drugs.

Drug	Effects
cannabis	Feel relaxed and happy. May make you see things that are not there. May prevent men from making sperm. Can cause bronchitis and lung cancer.
amphetamines	Feel alert, confident and cheerful. Don't want to eat. Can cause depression. Dangerous for people with heart problems.
ecstasy	Feel energetic and happy. Can make you depressed and lose your memory. Unable to sleep. Don't want to eat. Overheating while dancing can kill you.
heroin	Feel warm and relaxed. Regular use can stop you from going to the toilet. Highly addictive. Can make you more likely to catch diseases.

b Describe the effects of each of the four drugs listed in the table.

How do drugs affect the body?

If you take too much of a drug it will have side effects. Side effects can damage your body for good. They can even kill you.

Many drugs are **addictive**. If you stop taking them you feel bad and want some more of the drug. A drug addict needs to keep taking the drugs just to feel normal. Many addicts die from the drug's side effects.

c What does addictive mean?

How does alcohol affect the body?

Alcohol is a drug that is in wine, beer and spirits. People have drunk alcohol for hundreds of years. In small quantities it gives us a feeling of happiness and is quite pleasant. But even small quantities can have side effects.

- It makes you do things you would not normally do.
- It makes you lose your balance.
- It blurs your eyesight and speech.
- It makes you sleepy.
- It makes you lose water and become thirsty.
- It makes you react to things more slowly.

d Explain why you should not drink alcohol and drive a car.

Alcohol can also have serious long-term effects. It can damage your liver, which can kill you.

e Why should you not drink too much alcohol each week?

QUESTIONS

Copy these sentences and fill in the spaces using the words below:

  addictive change side effects

Drugs _____ the way your body works. Even drugs like alcohol can have serious _____. Some drugs are _____ and make you feel bad when you stop taking them.

KEY POINTS

- Drugs change the way your body works.
- All drugs have side effects.

Fit and healthy

B4 MOVEMENT AND EXERCISE

What is the job of the skeleton?

Your skeleton is made of bone. It holds your body up and protects some of the organs inside your body.

a What job does the skeleton do?

If your skeleton was made of a single bone you would not be able to move. Because it is made of lots of bones, you can move almost every part of your body.

The bones are held together at joints. It is the joints that allow the bones to move.

Hinge joints allow bones to move backwards and forwards like a door hinge. The elbow joint is a hinge joint.

Ball and socket joints allow the bones to move in all directions. There is a ball on the end of your thigh bone. It fits into a socket in your pelvis. This makes up the hip joint.

b Name an example of a hinge joint and a ball and socket joint.

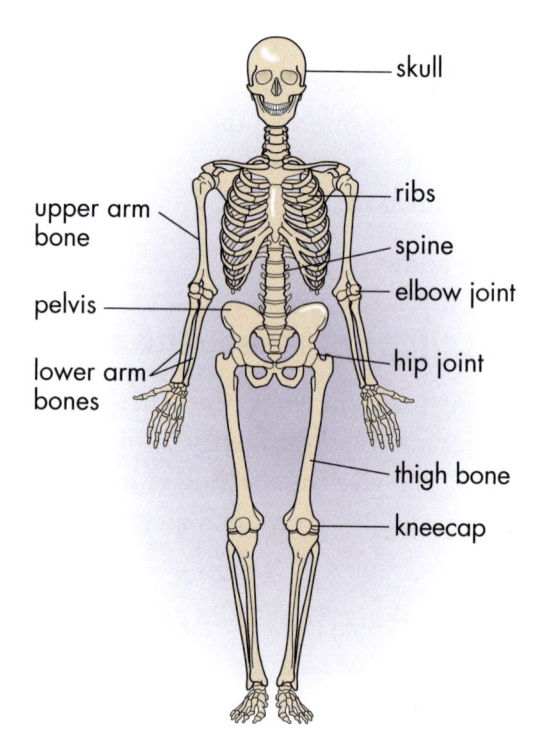

How do joints work?

Look at this diagram of a hip joint. It tells you what the different parts of a joint are called and what job they do.

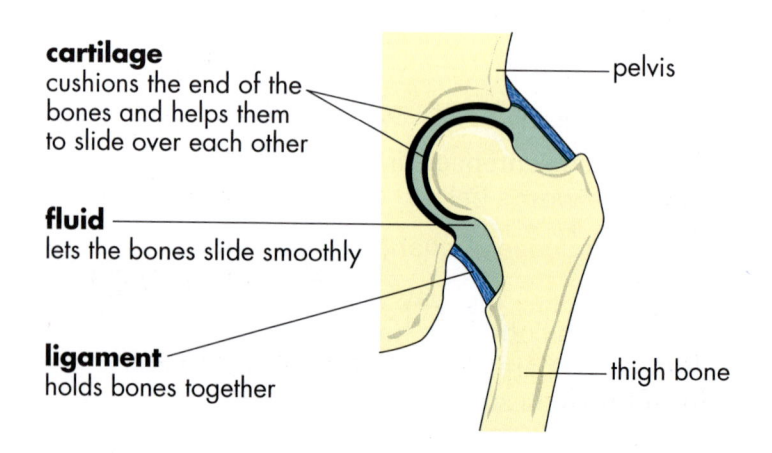

cartilage cushions the end of the bones and helps them to slide over each other

fluid lets the bones slide smoothly

ligament holds bones together

Fit and healthy

What do muscles do?

Muscles move bones. To do this muscles can only pull. They cannot push. So every joint needs two muscles – one to pull the bone one way, and another to pull it back again. Muscles pull by **contracting** or getting shorter.

Look at the picture of an arm.

- When the biceps muscle contracts it pulls the lower arm upwards. This stretches the triceps.

- When the triceps muscle contracts it pulls the lower arm downwards. This stretches the biceps.

The biceps and the triceps work together. When one contracts, the other relaxes. Because each one pulls the arm in opposite directions, they are called an **antagonistic pair**.

C What do we call muscles that pull in opposite directions?

What can go wrong with muscles?

A **strain** happens when we damage the muscle by a sudden awkward movement.

A **sprain** happens when we damage the ligament that holds the joint together.

How long will our joints last?

As people get older their joints tend to wear out. We call this arthritis. Some joints can be replaced with artificial ones in an operation.

Look at the picture. It shows an artificial hip joint.

QUESTIONS

Copy these sentences and write **true** or **false** next to each one:

Your skeleton holds your body up and protects some of your organs.

Joints hold the bones together and stop them from moving.

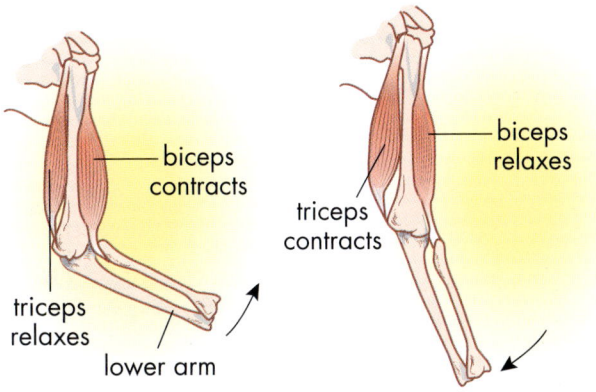

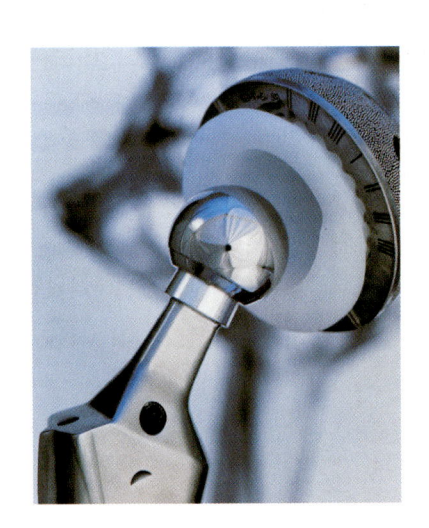

KEY POINTS

- Your skeleton holds your body up and protects some of your organs.

- Your bones are held together by joints that allow you to move.

Fit and healthy

C Plants and photosynthesis

C1 HOW DO PLANTS GROW?

What is photosynthesis?

Since you were born you have been getting bigger. You will keep on growing until you are an adult.

Plants also grow. You saw in Unit 7A how a tiny young redwood tree can grow into one of the tallest trees in the world.

People used to think that plants grew by taking materials in from the ground. We now know that plants grow by making their own food. We call this process **photosynthesis**.

a How do plants grow?

How does photosynthesis work?

Plants need light, water and carbon dioxide for photosynthesis.

- Plants get light from the Sun. They use sunlight as a source of energy.
- They get water from the soil through their roots.
- They get carbon dioxide from the air. They take in the carbon dioxide through their leaves.

b Where do plants get these things for photosynthesis?
   i light   ii water   iii carbon dioxide

In photosynthesis plants produce glucose and oxygen. Glucose is a sugar.

Oxygen gas is given off by the leaves into the air.

Look at the picture. It shows some pondweed.

The pondweed has given off oxygen. The oxygen has collected in the top of the test tube.

Do you remember the test for oxygen? The gas in the test tube will relight a glowing splint. This proves that it is oxygen.

The word equation for photosynthesis is:

$$\text{carbon dioxide} + \text{water} \xrightarrow{\text{light energy}} \text{glucose} + \text{oxygen}$$

What happens if you give a plant more light?

If you give a plant more light, it will photosynthesise faster.

Look at the pictures.

The pondweed that is closer to the lamp makes more bubbles of oxygen. This is because it is getting more light.

Becca measured the amount of oxygen in a greenhouse over a period of 24 hours. The graph below shows her results.

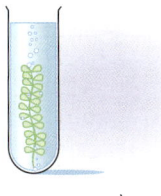

C When was the level of oxygen the highest?

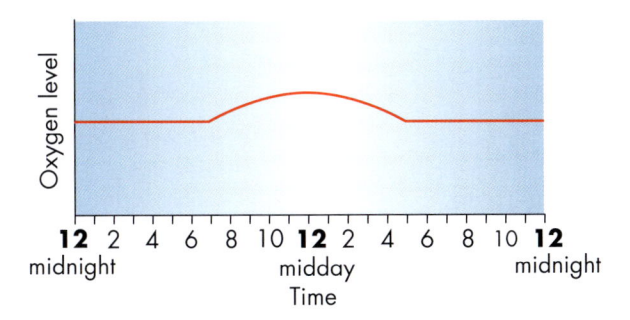

QUESTIONS

Copy this list of words. Write **P** beside each one that plants need for photosynthesis.

light   water   carbon dioxide   wind   oxygen

KEY POINTS

- Plants grow by making their own food. This is called photosynthesis.
- Photosynthesis goes more quickly if we give the plant more light.

Plants and photosynthesis

C2 WHAT IS THE ROLE OF THE LEAF IN PHOTOSYNTHESIS?

How is a leaf adapted for photosynthesis?

Look at the picture of a leaf.
It has veins to carry water for photosynthesis.
It is thin and broad to capture sunlight.

a How is a leaf adapted to carry out photosynthesis?

Even the inside of the leaf is adapted to help it carry out photosynthesis.

Look at the picture below. It shows what the inside of a leaf looks like under a microscope.

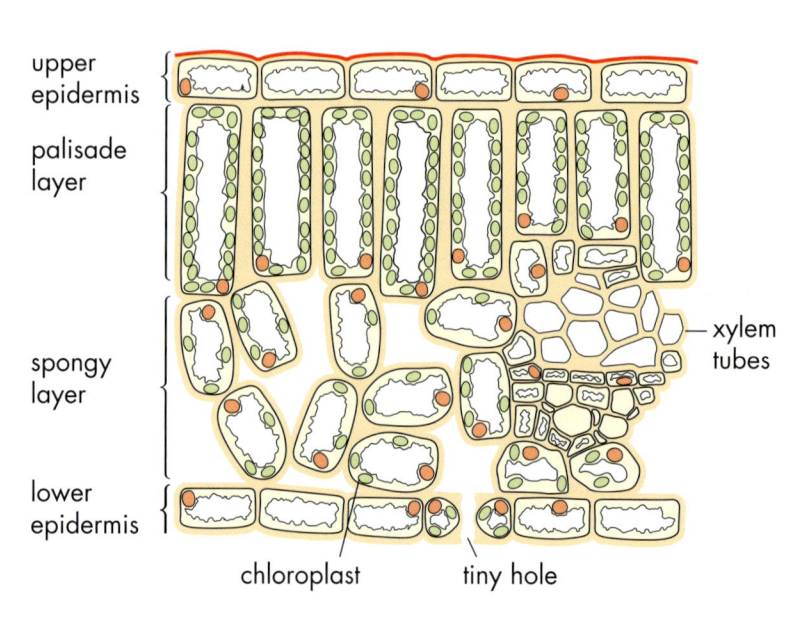

- The top layer is thin and clear to let light into the leaf.
- The palisade layer has chloroplasts. These contain green **chlorophyll**. This absorbs light energy from the Sun.
- The spongy layer has air spaces. These let carbon dioxide reach all the cells.
- The bottom layer has tiny holes. These let in carbon dioxide and let out oxygen.
- Xylem tubes carry water up from the roots to the leaf for photosynthesis.

b What job does chlorophyll do?

c What job do the tiny holes do?

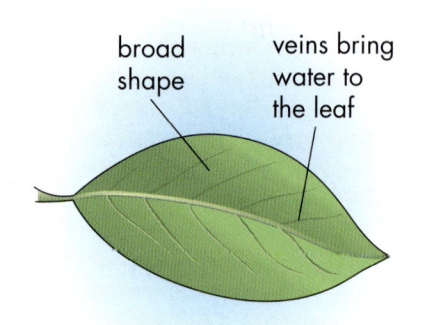

Plants and photosynthesis

Why are leaves green?

Leaves are green because they contain lots of chlorophyll. Without chlorophyll leaves cannot photosynthesise. They cannot make glucose. We can show this by doing an experiment.

Plants store glucose by turning it into starch. We can test a leaf for starch using iodine. If there is starch there the iodine turns black. This tells us the leaf has been photosynthesising.

Some leaves only have chlorophyll in parts of the leaf. Other parts are white.

If we test a leaf like this we find that starch is only there in the green parts, that contain chlorophyll.

Leaf before   Leaf after starch test

d Which parts of the leaf contain starch?

Why do leaves have different shapes?

Leaves that grow in the shade are often broader to catch more light.

Cactus leaves are spiky. They have a small surface so they lose less water. This is important for plants that live in a desert where there is not much water.

QUESTIONS

Copy these sentences choosing only the correct words:

Leaves / roots are adapted to do the job of photosynthesis. They contain chlorophyll that traps **energy / water** from sunlight. Cactus leaves are spiky to reduce **sunlight / water** loss.

KEY POINTS

- Leaves are adapted for photosynthesis.
- Chlorophyll is green and traps sunlight for photosynthesis.
- Leaves have different shapes in different environments.

C3 WHAT HAPPENS TO GLUCOSE PRODUCED IN THE LEAVES?

Where does a plant get its energy?

Here is the word equation for photosynthesis:

$$\text{carbon dioxide} + \text{water} \xrightarrow[\text{chlorophyll}]{\text{light energy}} \text{glucose} + \text{oxygen}$$

It shows how light energy becomes stored in the glucose.

Do you remember respiration? We use glucose in respiration.

$$\text{glucose} + \text{oxygen} \xrightarrow{\text{energy is released}} \text{carbon dioxide} + \text{water}$$

In respiration, we release energy from the glucose that we eat.

Plants respire just like we do. They make glucose by photosynthesis. Then they release some of the energy from the glucose, in respiration.

a Why do plants respire just like humans?

How do plants store glucose?

Most of the glucose that plants make is not used straight away for respiration. Instead they change it into starch and store it.

Look at the picture. It shows starch stored in a potato. Iodine was dropped on the potato. It has turned black, showing starch is there.

How does a plant grow?

Plants turn glucose into many other substances. They can turn glucose into fat or protein. They can use glucose to make a substance called cellulose.

Plants use these substances to make new cells. The more cells they have, the bigger they get. As plants get bigger they have more mass. We call this plant material **biomass**.

b What do we call plant material?

Look at the picture of the marrow. It is large and heavy. It has lots of biomass.

Plants store some food inside their seeds. When the seed grows it uses this stored food to make new cells.

Look at the picture of the bean seed. The root and shoot are growing, using food stored in the seed.

Later the bean will have new green leaves to carry out photosynthesis for itself.

How are plants useful?

Plants make all sorts of materials that we use, such as:

- wood for making furniture
- cotton fibre for making clothes
- food for eating.

These are all different kinds of biomass.

c What can humans use biomass for?

QUESTIONS

Copy these sentences and fill in the spaces using the words below:

glucose   respire   starch

Plants can photosynthesise and _____.
They convert the _____ they make into other substances such as _____, fat, protein or cellulose.

KEY POINTS

- Plants respire just like we do.
- Plants store glucose as starch, or turn it into many other useful substances.

C4 WHAT IS THE ROLE OF THE ROOT IN PHOTOSYNTHESIS?

Why do plants need water?

1. Plants need water for photosynthesis.
2. Water makes plants firm. Without water they wilt and go floppy.
3. Water helps plants to keep cool, just as sweating keeps us cool.
4. Water helps to transport nutrients around the plant.

a Why do plants need water?

How are roots adapted to absorb water?

Plants absorb water through their roots.

Roots are branched. This means they can touch more soil and absorb more water.

Roots have root hair cells growing out from the root. These also mean they can absorb more water.

b Why do roots have lots of branches and fine root hairs?

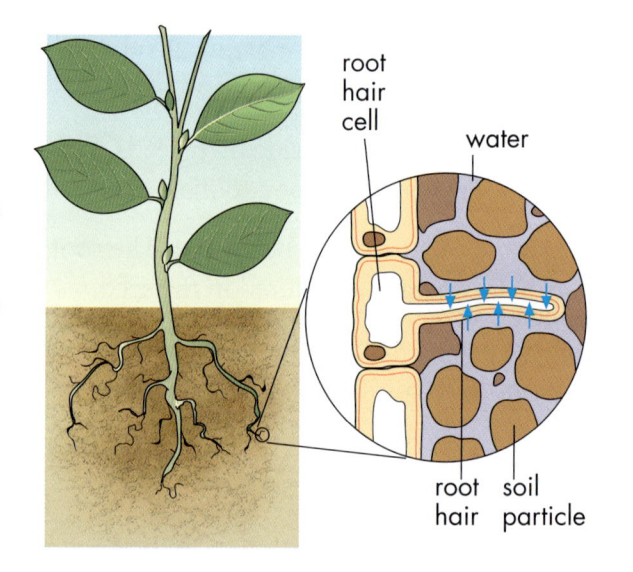

How does water travel in a plant?

Water goes into the plant through the roots. It is carried up the stem and into the leaf.

The water is carried in small tubes called xylem. Xylem tubes run through the veins in a plant.

You can see the xylem in the veins by carrying out a simple experiment.

If you stand a stick of celery in red ink, the ink is carried up the stem to the leaves. By cutting across the stem we can see the xylem stained red by the ink.

The veins go all the way up the plant into the leaves.

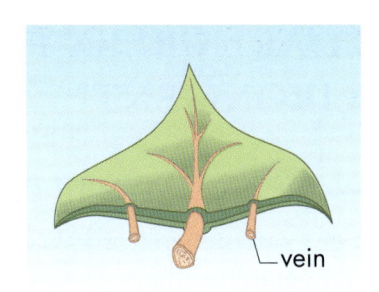

Why do plants need nutrients?

Plant roots do not only absorb water. They also absorb nutrients. Just as we need vitamins, plants need nutrients to stay healthy. Plants need:

- nitrogen to make protein for growth

Without nitrogen the plant grows slowly and its leaves are small and pale.

- phosphorus to make roots

Without phosphorus the roots are small and the leaves are purple.

- potassium to make flowers

Without potassium there are no flowers and the leaf edges turn yellow.

- magnesium to make chlorophyll.

Without magnesium the plant is yellow and cannot photosynthesise.

QUESTIONS

Copy these sentences choosing only the correct words:

Animals / plants need water for photosynthesis. The **roots / stems** have branches and fine root hair cells to absorb more water. The water then travels up the plant through **phloem / xylem** vessels.

KEY POINTS

- Plants need water for photosynthesis.
- Roots are branched and have root hair cells to help them absorb more water.
- Water travels up the plant through xylem vessels.

C5 WHY ARE GREEN PLANTS IMPORTANT IN THE ENVIRONMENT?

What affects oxygen and carbon dioxide levels in the air?

Plants give out oxygen from photosynthesis. Animals need oxygen to breathe.

Animals give out carbon dioxide. Plants need carbon dioxide for photosynthesis.

When everything is in balance, the levels of these two gases in the air should stay the same.

- Photosynthesis puts oxygen into the air. It takes out carbon dioxide.
- Respiration puts carbon dioxide into the air. It takes out oxygen.

a What takes carbon dioxide out of the air?

b What puts carbon dioxide into the air?

Why are the levels of oxygen and carbon dioxide changing?

Today we are burning more fuel than ever before. Like respiration, burning fuel puts carbon dioxide into the air.

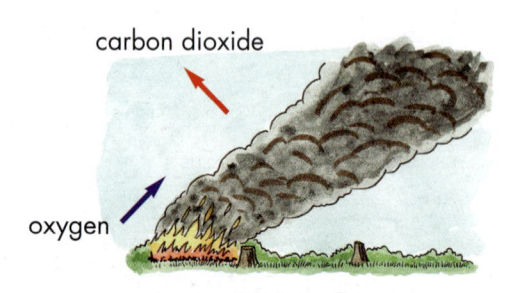

Plants and photosynthesis

Why are rainforests important?

C5

Plants are very important. They remove carbon dioxide and provide us with oxygen. But we are cutting down large areas of forest.

Rainforests cover huge areas in hot damp regions of the world. Rainforests contain lots of different plants.

Over the last 50 years, people have cut down vast areas of rainforest. They use the wood for making paper and furniture and for building.

Unfortunately the trees and plants are not being replaced. This means that less carbon dioxide is being taken out of the air. It also means less oxygen is being produced.

Scientists are very worried about this. It makes carbon dioxide levels in the air rise, and oxygen levels fall.

C Why is more carbon dioxide going into the air?

QUESTIONS

Copy these sentences and fill in the spaces using the words below:

> carbon dioxide   cut   rainforest

The _____ level in the air is rising. To stop this happening we need the _____. But it is being _____ down to provide wood for furniture and for building.

KEY POINTS

- Carbon dioxide levels in the air are rising.
- Oxygen levels in the air are falling.
- Rainforests are being cut down. But they are needed to keep the balance between oxygen and carbon dioxide.

Plants and photosynthesis

D Plants for food

D1 WHERE DOES OUR FOOD COME FROM?

Where do humans fit into a food web?

Humans eat many different animals and plants. This means we are part of lots of different **food chains**. If we put these food chains together, we get a **food web**.

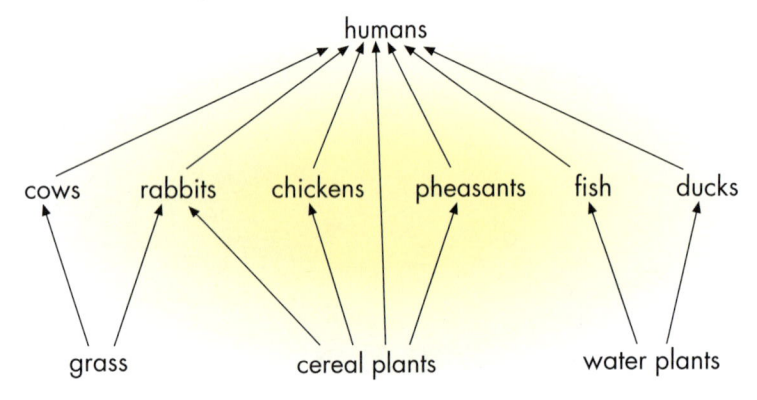

Plants use energy from the Sun to produce food. Plants are called **producers**.

Animals cannot photosynthesise. They eat or consume food. This is why animals are called **consumers**.

There are three types of consumer:
- **Herbivores** are animals that only eat plants.
- **Carnivores** are animals that only eat other animals.
- **Omnivores** are animals that eat both plants and animals.

Humans are omnivores. We eat both plants and animals.

a Why are humans called omnivores?

These crop plants are producing food for us to eat.

Where do plants store food?

Plants make glucose by photosynthesis. They do not use all the glucose for respiration. Some is left over.

Plants turn this glucose into other substances such as starch, fat and protein. This food is stored in different parts of the plant.

Look at the picture. It shows some of the places that plants can store food.

b **List some of the places that plants can store food.**

leaf
roots
stems
fruits
seeds

Potatoes store food as starch. Look at the picture. If you drop iodine onto a potato, it turns black. This shows that the potato has starch stored in it.

c **How do potatoes store food?**

Why do plants store food?

There are three main reasons why plants store food:

1. To survive the winter. Leaves usually drop off in the winter and the plants cannot photosynthesise. They use stored food for respiration during the winter.

2. For seeds. When seeds start to grow they cannot photosynthesise until they have green leaves. The stored food keeps the seed going until it makes green leaves of its own.

3. To make sweet-tasting fruit. Animals like to eat the fruit. They spread the seeds that are inside the fruit. The seeds come out in the animal's droppings ready to start to grow.

d **Why do plants store food?**

QUESTIONS

Copy these sentences choosing only the correct words:

Plants are called **consumers / producers** because they produce food. Humans are called **omnivores / producers** because we eat plants and animals. Plants **do not store / store** food in leaves, stems and roots.

KEY POINTS

- Humans are part of a food web.
- Plants store some of their food.

Plants for food

D2 HOW DO FERTILISERS AFFECT PLANT GROWTH?

What do fertilisers contain?

Fertilisers contain nutrients that plants need to stay healthy. They contain nitrates, phosphates, potassium and magnesium.

The picture shows some of the plant nutrients found in fertiliser.

NPK Fertiliser	15-5-30
Nitrogen (N)	15%
Ammoniacal	3.7%
Nitrate	11.3%
Phosphorus Pentoxide (P_2O_5)	5% (P2.2%)
Potassium Oxide (K_2O)	30% (K24.9%)
Magnesium (MgO)	3% (Mg1.8%)
Boron (B)	0.025%
Copper (Cu) EDTA	0.010%
Iron (Fe) EDTA	0.070%
Manganese (Mn) EDTA	0.040%
Molybdenum (Mo)	0.004%
Zinc (Zn) EDTA	0.025%

a Name two plant nutrients found in fertiliser.

Fertiliser labels show an **application rate**. This tells the farmer how much to use.

b What does application rate mean?

Why do farmers use fertiliser?

Using fertiliser can be very expensive. First farmers pay for the fertiliser. Then they need machinery to spread it. Finally they pay the person who spreads the fertiliser.

So why does the farmer bother to use fertiliser?

Fertilisers make plants grow bigger. So the farmer can harvest more crop. The farmer gets more money from selling this bigger crop. It pays for using the fertiliser, with some extra left over.

c Why do farmers use expensive fertilisers?

Some farmers save money by using manure. Manure is the faeces produced by animals. Like fertiliser, manure contains lots of nutrients that the plants need.

d Why do some farmers use manure?

Why do plants grow better with fertilisers?

Fertilisers dissolve in water. The plant roots absorb the water containing the fertiliser. The nutrients are then transported all round the plant.

The table shows what you learnt about plant nutrients in Unit C4.

Nutrient	Why the plant needs it
nitrogen	to make protein for growth
phosphorus	to make roots
potassium	to make flowers
magnesium	to make chlorophyll

Apart from the four nutrients in the table, plants also need other nutrients in very small amounts. These are called **trace elements**.

The table shows what happens if a plant does not get enough trace elements.

Nutrient	What happens without it
iron	yellow leaves
copper	brown spots, leaves die
molybdenum	narrow leaves

e Name three trace elements that plants need.

QUESTIONS

Copy these sentences and fill in the spaces using the words below:

crop   magnesium   nutrients   trace

Fertilisers contain nitrates, phosphates, potassium and _____ . These are essential _____ needed by the plants. Farmers use fertilisers to increase the yield of their _____ . Fertilisers also contain _____ elements.

KEY POINTS

- Fertilisers contain nutrients that plants need.
- Farmers use fertilisers to increase the yield of their crop.

Plants for food

D3 HOW DOES COMPETITION AFFECT PLANT GROWTH?

What are weeds?

Farmers and gardeners hate weeds. A **weed** is a plant growing where it is not wanted.

Look at the picture of a farmer's field of wheat. Some weeds are growing in the field.

a What are the weeds growing in the wheat field?

Farmers don't like weeds because they reduce the yield of the crop.

Look at the two graphs.

At Manor farm people pull out the weeds.

At Oak farm they just leave the weeds to grow.

b Which farm has the bigger crop yield?

Oak farm has a smaller crop yield because the weeds steal nutrients from the crop plants.

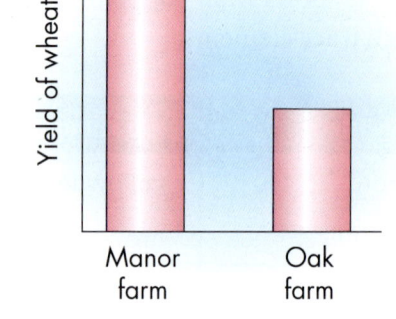

How do weeds compete for resources?

Weeds steal these resources from crop plants:

- nutrients from the soil
- water from the soil
- carbon dioxide from the air
- sunlight for photosynthesis.

When two different plants need the same resources we say they are **competing** for the resources.

Some weeds compete by growing very tall and getting all the sunlight.

c What resource are these very tall weeds competing for?

Plants for food

How do farmers kill weeds?

On a large farm it would be impossible to pull up every weed by hand. It would take a long time and need lots of people. It is much cheaper and quicker to use chemicals called **weedkillers**.

Different weedkillers contain different chemicals. They kill weeds in different ways.

Weedkillers are **selective**. This means that each weedkiller kills some weeds but not the crop. So the farmer can spray the weedkiller on the crop.

Spraying crops with weedkiller.

d What does 'selective weedkiller' mean?

Is killing weeds always a good idea?

Unfortunately, killing weeds can affect other living things. Fat hen is a weed that grows in sugar beet fields. Skylarks and partridges eat it.

Look at the food web. If the farmer kills the fat hen plants then there will be fewer skylarks and partridges.

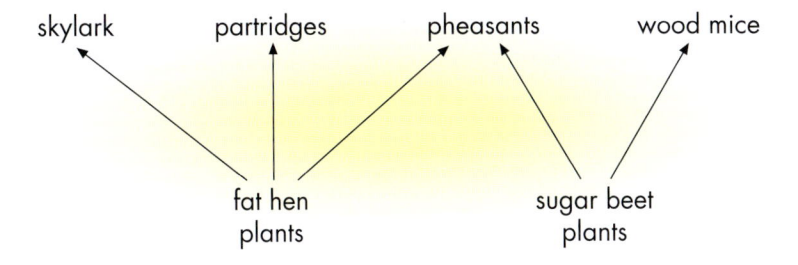

QUESTIONS

Copy these sentences and fill in the spaces using the words below:

compete   weedkillers   resources   weeds

Plants that grow where they are not wanted are called _____. They _____ with other plants for _____. Farmers kill them with _____.

KEY POINTS

- Weeds are plants growing where they are not wanted.
- They compete with crops for resources so farmers kill them with weedkillers.

Plants for food

D4 HOW DO PESTS AFFECT PLANT GROWTH?

What are pests?

Pests are animals that feed on farmers' crops.

Look at the pictures. They are all pests.

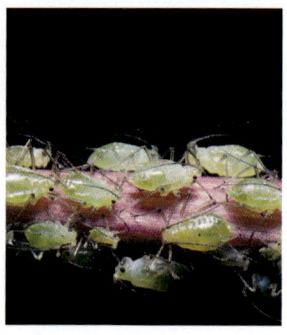

Crops are plants that are grown for people to eat. When pests eat these crops they are competing with people for food.

Look at the food web. Mice are competing with humans for wheat and barley.

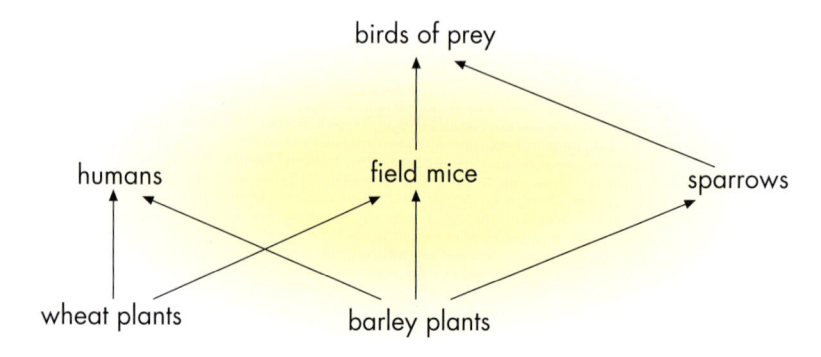

a What else is competing with humans for barley?

How do farmers kill pests?

Farmers use chemicals called **pesticides** to kill pests.

- **Insecticides** kill insects.
- Slug pellets kill slugs and snails. These taste nice to slugs and snails. But they contain a poisonous chemical, so the slugs and snails die.

b What do we call chemicals that kill pests?

Is killing pests always a good idea?

Birds eat some insect pests. If the farmer kills the insects, the birds have less food to eat.

Look at the pyramids of numbers. Before spraying there are lots of insects, but also lots of blue tits. After spraying there are less insect pests. But there are also less blue tits.

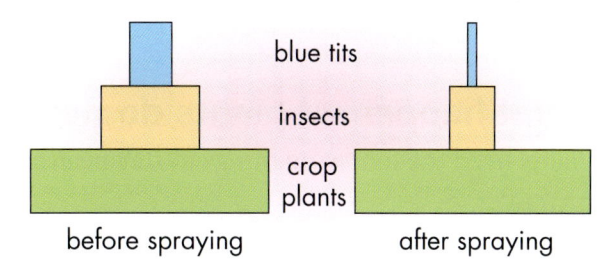

How does DDT build up in food chains?

Some pesticides break down after a short period of time. They disappear from the plants and soil.

Other pesticides do not break down. They stay in the environment for many years. One pesticide like this is called DDT.

DDT is very good at killing insects. Imagine you spray a rose bush with DDT to kill some greenfly.

- Most greenfly die. But some only get a little DDT and manage to survive.
- Blue tits eat these greenfly. Each greenfly gives them a small amount of DDT. Blue tits eat lots of greenfly so they get quite a lot of DDT.
- Sparrow hawks eat the blue tits. Just a few blue tits contain enough DDT to kill the sparrow hawk.

QUESTIONS

Copy these sentences and write **true** or **false** next to each one:
Pests eat food grown for humans to eat.
Pesticides are chemicals that save pests.
Using pesticides reduces the food supply for birds.

KEY POINTS

- Pests are animals that eat food grown for humans.
- Farmers kill pests using pesticides. But this has an effect on the food web.

Plants for food

D5 WHAT IS THE PERFECT ENVIRONMENT FOR GROWING PLANTS?

What happens if plants do not get what they need?

Plants need the following things to stay healthy:

- light
- water
- nutrients
- warmth
- carbon dioxide.

We can prove this by taking each one away in turn and seeing what happens to the plant. Look back at page 27 to see what happens when plants do not get the nutrients that they need.

No light: pale, thin and spindly.

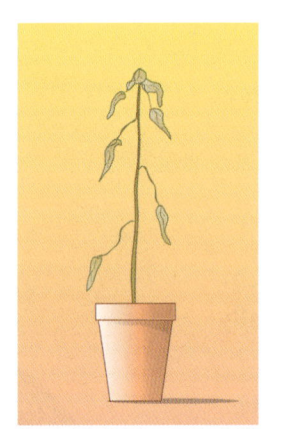

No water: leaves dry, the plant has gone limp and died.

Cold: some plants cannot survive outside in winter.

No carbon dioxide: cannot photosynthesise.

a What happens when a plant has no light?

b What happens when a plant has no water?

How do greenhouses help plants to grow?

In a greenhouse, the farmer can control the environment. They can control the temperature and the amount of light, water, nutrients and carbon dioxide that the plants get. It is also much easier to control the weeds.

38 Plants for food

How do greenhouses work?

- To control light, you can put shades in the windows.
- To control the temperature, you use heaters when it is cold, and windows that open automatically when it gets too hot.
- To control water, there is a computer-controlled watering system. It measures the amount of water in the soil and gives the plants the right amount of water.
- To control nutrients, fertilisers are used when they are needed.
- Extra carbon dioxide can be pumped into the greenhouse to make sure plants have enough for photosynthesis.

C How is temperature controlled in a greenhouse?

How can we farm without destroying the environment?

It is important that by growing crops we do not destroy the environment. Farmers can do this by:

1. using other insects like ladybirds to eat pests rather than using pesticides
2. keeping hedgerows to provide a home for the birds and useful insects that eat pests
3. using people to remove weeds rather than using weedkillers.

Farmers that use these methods are called **organic farmers**.

QUESTIONS

1. Write down three ways that greenhouses help farmers to grow food.
2. Write down three ways that farmers can help to protect the environment

KEY POINTS

- In a greenhouse, farmers can control the growing environment.
- Organic farmers do not destroy the environment.

E Reactions of metals and metal compounds

E1 WHY ARE METALS USEFUL?

What are metals?

There are many different metals. The pictures show just three of them.

Potassium   Sodium   Lead

Most metals have certain things in common.

Look at the table. It shows the properties of most metals.

Property: metals are …	Meaning
strong	difficult to break
shiny and silver	reflect light and most are silvery coloured
hard	difficult to scratch with a nail
flexible	bend without breaking
dense	very heavy for their size
tough	do not break when you hit them
solid	not liquid or gas
good thermal conductors	allow heat to pass through easily
good electrical conductors	allow electricity to pass through easily

When is a metal not a metal?

There are always exceptions to every rule:
- Gold and copper are metals, but they are not silver.
- Mercury is a metal, but it is a liquid not a solid.
- Graphite is *not* a metal, but it will conduct electricity.

a Why are mercury and gold not like most other metals?

What are non-metals like?

Non-metals are elements that are not metals. Most non-metals are weak, soft and easy to break. They are usually lighter than metals for their size. They don't conduct heat and electricity very well. Many of them are gases.

b How are non-metals different from metals?

What are metals used for?

Metals have thousands of uses. They are used to make coins, spaceships and cooking pots. Different metals have different properties. This means that different metals are suitable for different jobs.

- Copper is a good conductor of electricity. This is why it is used to make electrical wires. Aluminium is also good at conducting electricity. Because it is lighter than copper it is used to make overhead electric cables.
- Iron is strong and hard. It is also very cheap. This is why it is used for making bridges.

c Why is iron used for making bridges?

QUESTIONS

Copy these sentences choosing only the correct words:

Metals are **bad / good** conductors of heat and electricity. They have **the same / different** properties which means they can be used for **the same / different** jobs.

KEY POINTS

- Different metals have different properties and uses.

Reactions of metals and metal compounds

E2 HOW DO METALS REACT WITH ACIDS?

Which metals react with acids?

Some metals react with acids very quickly. Others do not react at all.

Zinc reacts quickly with acids.

Gold does not react at all with acids.

a Which metal reacts quickly with acids?

b Which metal does not react with acids at all?

What is made when metals react with acids?

Look at the top picture of zinc in acid. It is giving off bubbles. This tells us that a chemical change is happening. The bubbles are a gas called hydrogen.

c How do we know that a chemical change is taking place when zinc is put in acid?

How do we know the bubbles are hydrogen? You may remember that hydrogen burns very quickly. If we collect a test tube of hydrogen, we can light it. It burns with a squeaky pop.

When an acid reacts with a metal, a **salt** is made as well as hydrogen.

metal + acid ⟶ salt + hydrogen

What is a salt?

We think of salt as a white substance that we sprinkle on chips. But there are many different kinds of salt.

A salt is made when a metal reacts with an acid. Different acids and different metals will produce different salts.

Look at the picture below.

Zinc is added to sulphuric acid. Hydrogen is given off. Zinc sulphate is formed. Zinc sulphate is a salt.

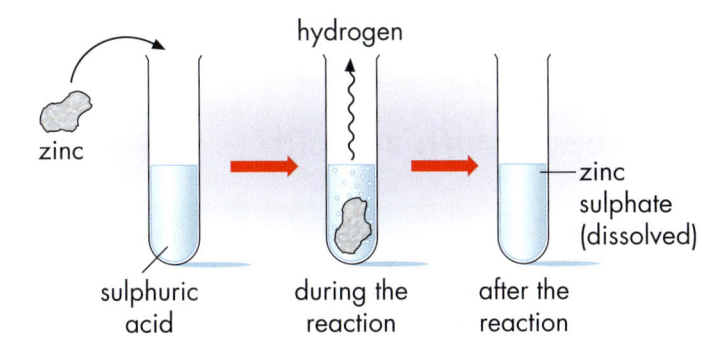

d What is made when a metal reacts with an acid?

How are these reactions useful?

Zinc sulphate is used to make many different things. It used to make synthetic fibres for clothes, like the ones shown in the picture. It is also used in pesticides.

QUESTIONS

Copy these sentences and fill in the spaces using the words below:

      gold   salt   hydrogen   zinc

_____ reacts with acids but _____ does not. When metals react with acids they give off _____ gas and make a _____ .

KEY POINTS

- Some metals react with acid, others do not.
- A metal reacts with an acid to form a salt and hydrogen.

Reactions of metals and metal compounds

E3 HOW DO CARBONATES REACT WITH ACIDS?

What is a carbonate?

Limestone is calcium carbonate. These cliffs are made of limestone.

There are other carbonates too, such as sodium carbonate and magnesium carbonate.

Metal carbonates are **bases**. Bases are the opposite of acids. All alkalis are bases.

a What is a base?

What is made when a carbonate reacts with an acid?

Look at the picture. It shows calcium carbonate reacting with hydrochloric acid. Three new substances are made during this reaction.

- Bubbles of gas are given off. The gas is carbon dioxide. It dissolves in the water.
- A salt is produced. It is called calcium chloride.
- Water is also made by the reaction.

All these changes tell us that a chemical reaction has taken place.

b How do we know that a chemical reaction has taken place when calcium carbonate is mixed with hydrochloric acid?

How do we know the bubbles are carbon dioxide? The picture shows how we can bubble the gas through limewater. The limewater turns milky. This shows that the gas is carbon dioxide.

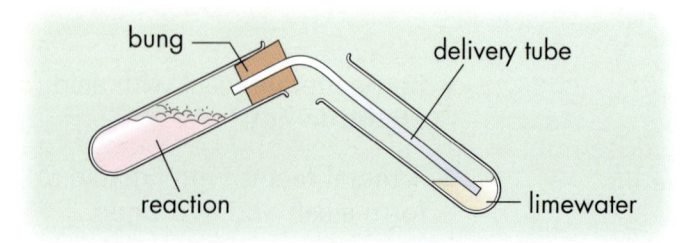

Whenever a carbonate reacts with an acid, a salt, carbon dioxide and water are made.

carbonate + acid ⟶ salt + carbon dioxide + water

The picture shows the reaction.

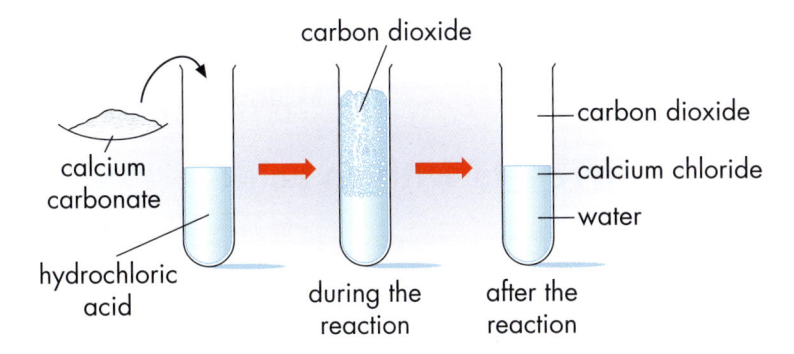

Which salt?

How can we work out which salt will be made? It is quite easy if we know the name of the acid and the name of the substance reacting with it.

- Hydro**chloric** acid always makes a **chloride** salt.
- **Sulphuric** acid always makes a **sulphate** salt.
- **Nitric** acid always makes a **nitrate** salt.

So …

Calcium carbonate added to hydro**chloric** acid makes **calcium chloride** salt.

Lead added to **sulphuric** acid makes **lead sulphate** salt.

c What salt will be made if we add <u>potassium</u> carbonate to <u>nitric</u> acid?

QUESTIONS

Copy these sentences and write **true** or **false** next to each one:

Carbonates react with acids to form a salt, carbon dioxide and water.

Hydrochloric acid always makes a sulphate salt.

Nitric acid always makes a nitrate salt.

KEY POINTS

- Carbonates react with acids to form a salt, carbon dioxide and water.

Reactions of metals and metal compounds

E4 HOW DO METAL OXIDES REACT WITH ACIDS?

What is a metal oxide?

Copper oxide is an example of a metal oxide. It is made from the metal copper joining with oxygen. Metal oxides are always bases, the opposite of acids.

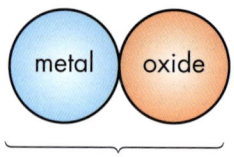

What is made when a metal oxide reacts with an acid?

Look at the picture. It shows what happens when black copper oxide reacts with sulphuric acid. Two new substances are made during this reaction.

- When a metal oxide reacts with an acid, a salt is produced. The salt in this reaction is called copper sulphate.
- Water is also made.

a What salt is made when copper oxide is mixed with sulphuric acid?

No gas is given off. But there is a change of colour. Copper oxide is black. Copper sulphate is blue. The colour change tells us that a chemical reaction has taken place.

b How do we know that a chemical reaction has taken place when we add copper oxide to sulphuric acid?

We can write a word equation to show what has happened in the reaction.

copper oxide + sulphuric acid ⟶ copper sulphate + water

c Apart from copper sulphate, what else is made during this reaction?

Getting the salt from the solution

If we gently heat the copper sulphate solution, the water will evaporate and just leave the copper sulphate salt behind.

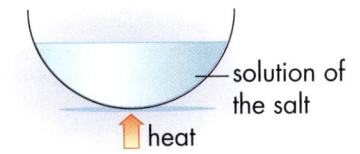

Copper sulphate makes a beautiful blue crystal.

How are these reactions useful?

Copper sulphate has many uses.

- It stops fungus growing on seeds.
- It preserves wood.
- Very tiny amounts are added to baby foods and vitamin pills as a preservative. (But it is poisonous in normal quantities so copper sulphate must never be eaten.)

QUESTIONS

Copy these sentences and fill in the spaces using the words below:

      metal oxides   sulphate   water

_____ react with acid to produce a salt plus _____. Copper oxide reacts with sulphuric acid to produce copper _____ and water.

KEY POINTS

- When metal oxides react with acids they produce a salt plus water.

Reactions of metals and metal compounds

E5 HOW DO ALKALIS REACT WITH ACIDS?

What are alkalis?

Alkalis are bases. Bases are the opposite of acids. Alkalis are bases that will dissolve in water.

Alkalis have a pH number higher than 7. Remember that acids have a pH number lower than 7.

You may have seen the alkalis potassium hydroxide and sodium hydroxide in your school laboratory.

a Name an alkali that you have seen in your school laboratory.

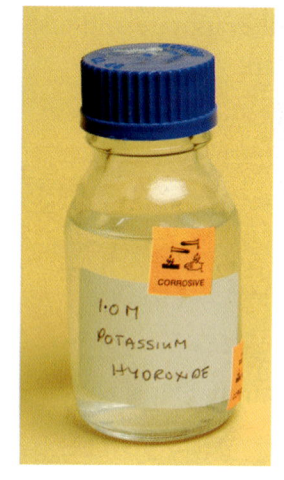

Potassium hydroxide solution.

Alkalis and safety

Most people think that acids are dangerous. But alkalis are even more dagerous.

Alkalis react very easily with your skin. They are also much harder to wash off if you spill them on you.

If an alkali splashes into your eye it will be very painful. It could even blind you.

b Which are more dangerous, acids or alkalis?

c Why should you always wear safety specs when using acids and alkalis?

Neutralisation

Neutralisation happens when an acid reacts with an alkali. When the acid and the alkali exactly cancel out, they produce a neutral solution. This is neither acidic or alkaline. It has pH 7.

d What pH is neutral?

Look at the picture. It shows this experiment. Small amounts of acid are added to the alkali until it is neutral.

The point at which the solution becomes neutral is called the **end point**.

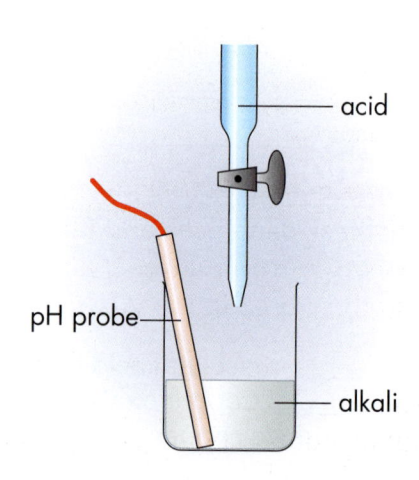

Reactions of metals and metal compounds

Look at the table. It shows the pH of the mixture as hydrochloric acid is added to an alkali.

Amount of hydrochloric acid added in cm³	1	2	3	4	5	6	7	8	9	9.5	10	10.5	11	12	13	14	15
pH of mixture	14	14	14	14	14	14	14	14	14	12	7	2.5	1	1	1	1	1

e How much hydrochloric acid was added to give a pH of 7?

What is made when alkalis react with acids?

Two new substances are made when an alkali and an acid neutralise each other:

- a salt is always made
- water is always made.

When potassium hydroxide reacts with hydrochloric acid, a salt called potassium chloride is made.

potassium hydroxide + hydrochloric acid ⟶ potassium chloride + water

f What is made when an acid reacts with an alkali?

How are these reactions useful?

We use neutralisation reactions to treat insect stings and indigestion. These reactions also make salts that are used in gunpowder and in washing powders.

Gunpowder

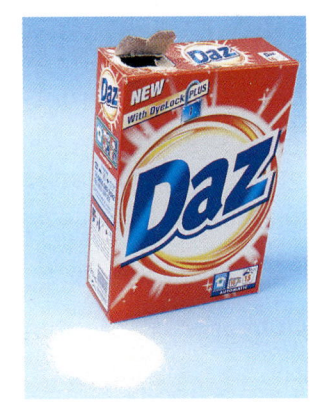

Washing powder

QUESTIONS

Copy these sentences and fill in the spaces using the words below:

salt   acids   neutral

Alkalis react with _____ to make a _____ solution containing a _____ and water.

KEY POINTS

- Alkalis react with acids to make a neutral solution containing a salt and water.

Reactions of metals and metal compounds

E6 BALANCED EQUATIONS

What happens in a reaction?

We have already looked at the reaction between zinc metal and sulphuric acid on page 43.

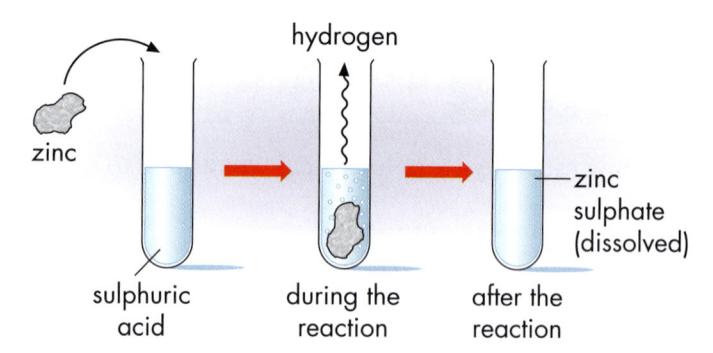

This is the word equation:

zinc + sulphuric acid ⟶ zinc sulphate + hydrogen

Here is a 'particle picture'.

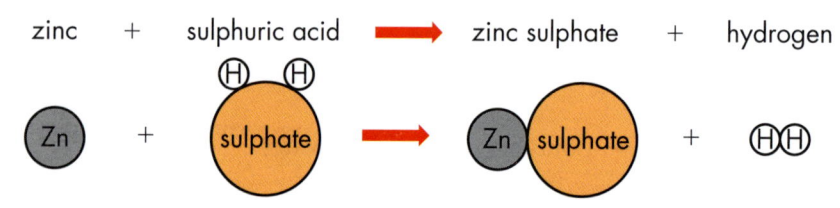

This picture shows how the groups of atoms have been rearranged to make new substances.

Why should equations be balanced?

Remember that atoms are not created or destroyed in a reaction. They are just rearranged. This means that there must be the same number of zinc atoms or hydrogen atoms on both sides of the equation. They have just been rearranged.

a What happens to the atoms during a reaction?

Look at the reaction between zinc and sulphuric acid again. The 'sulphate particle' is really made up of sulphur and four oxygens:

Reactions of metals and metal compounds

You can see that four different kinds of atom are involved.

b How many kinds of atoms are involved in this reaction?

If we count the numbers of atoms that are used in the reaction, we find:

Zn atoms	1
H atoms	2
S atoms	1
O atoms	4
Total	8

If we count the numbers of atoms in the products of the reaction, we find:

Zn atoms	1
H atoms	2
S atoms	1
O atoms	4
Total	8

You can see that there are exactly the same number of each kind of atom on both sides of the equation. As both the numbers are the same, we say the equation is **balanced**.

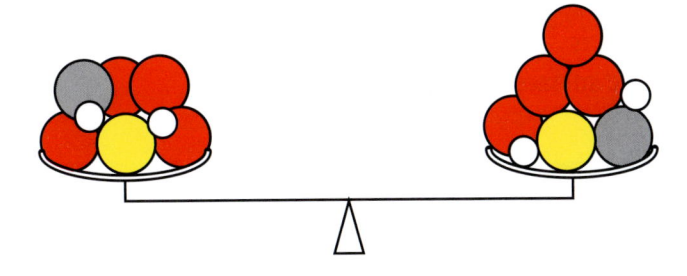

QUESTIONS

Copy these sentences choosing only the correct words:

Equations are **balanced / not balanced** when the number and type of atoms are the same on both sides of the equation.

Equations must **always / never** be balanced.

KEY POINTS

- Equations must always be balanced.
- This means there are the same numbers of each type of atom on both sides of the equation. They are just rearranged.

Reactions of metals and metal compounds

F Patterns of reactivity

F1 WHAT MAKES METALS CHANGE?

How are metals affected by air and water?

When you put metals into acids, some of them react quicker than others.

In the same way some metals react with the air quicker than others.

Gold never reacts with the air.

Iron reacts with the air in only a few days.

When a metal starts to react with the air, it becomes less shiny.

We say that the metal has become **tarnished**. When iron becomes tarnished it turns to rust.

Gold stays shiny and bright.

Iron rusts.

a What does iron turn to when it is tarnished?

Look at the pictures of the metal lithium. When it is freshly cut it looks silver. But 60 seconds later the surface has tarnished.

Freshly cut lithium.

60 seconds later.

b What colour is freshly cut lithium?

Do metals react with oxygen?

The freshly cut lithium reacts with the oxygen in the air.

c Which metal reacts the fastest with the oxygen in the air: gold, iron or lithium?

d Which metal never reacts with oxygen in the air: gold, iron or lithium?

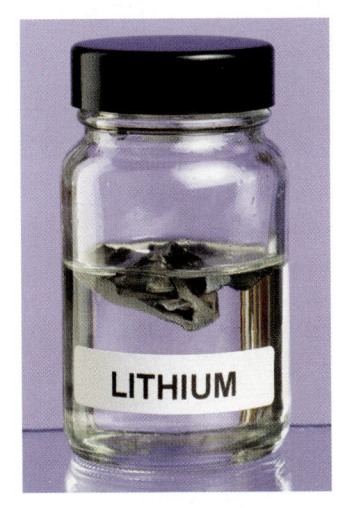

We keep lithium in a jar of oil to keep it fresh. The oil stops it reacting with the oxygen in the air.

Putting metals in order of reactivity

By comparing how quickly the three metals react with oxygen, we can put them into an order. The one that reacts the most slowly goes at the bottom of the list. The one that reacts the most quickly goes at the top. Scientists call this list the **reactivity series**.

e What is the name for a list of metals, written in order of how quickly they react?

f List gold, iron and lithium in order of reactivity, with the quickest at the top.

Scientist don't just list three metals. They include many more metals in their reactivity series. The series helps us to compare different metals.

QUESTIONS

Copy these sentences choosing only the correct words:

Gold reacts **quickly / not at all** with the oxygen in the air. Some metals like lithium react very **quickly / slowly** with oxygen. Scientists put metals into an order of reactivity. They call it the reactivity **list / series**.

KEY POINTS

- Different metals react at different speeds with the oxygen in the air.
- Gold does not react with the oxygen in the air at all.

Patterns of reactivity

F2 HOW DO METALS REACT WITH WATER?

Do metals react with cold water?

Some metals react if we put them in cold water. Look at the picture. It shows lithium reacting with cold water and giving off a gas.

It takes just a few minutes for the lithium to completely react with the water.

Some metals react even quicker with cold water. Look at the picture. It shows potassium reacting with cold water. The reaction is very fast and the gas it gives off is burning.

a Which reacts quicker with cold water, lithium or potassium?

The metals react with the water to form a **hydroxide**. Lithium makes lithium hydroxide and potassium makes potassium hydroxide.

All hydroxides are bases. If the hydroxide dissolves it is an alkali.

b If we put universal indicator in the water after potassium had finished reacting, would it show an acid or alkali?

When a metal reacts with water, the gas given off is hydrogen. Here is a word equation for the reaction:

metal + water ⟶ metal hydroxide + hydrogen

Magnesium is a metal. It does not react with cold water. But it reacts very slowly in hot water.

c What gas will magnesium give off when it reacts with hot water?

Metals reacting with oxygen and water

Look at the table. It shows the reactivity series of metals with oxygen and also with water. Remember that the fastest metal is at the top.

Reactivity series for metal with oxygen	Reactivity series for metal with water
potassium	potassium
sodium	sodium
lithium	lithium
calcium	calcium
magnesium	magnesium
silver	silver
gold	gold

d What do you notice about the two reactivity series?

e Why do you think that people make jewellery out of silver and gold?

QUESTIONS

1. Name one metal that reacts quickly with water.
2. Name one metal that is less reactive than lithium.
3. Name one metal whose reactivity is between potassium and lithium.

KEY POINTS

- Some metals react with water.
- The reactivity series of metals is the same with oxygen and with water.

Patterns of reactivity

F3 DO ALL METALS REACT WITH ACIDS?

What is formed when metals react with acids?

When a metal reacts with an acid, hydrogen gas and a salt are always formed.

Look at the picture. It shows magnesium in hydrochloric acid.

When magnesium reacts with hydrochloric acid, the salt magnesium chloride is formed.

a What salt will be formed when calcium reacts with hydrochloric acid?

Look at the top picture again. When magnesium reacts with hydrochloric acid, bubbles of hydrogen gas are produced. We test for hydrogen with a lighted splint, as shown opposite.

b What gas will be produced when calcium reacts with hydrochloric acid?

Do all metals react in the same way?

Look at the following pictures. They show different metals reacting with dilute hydrochloric acid.

Calcium.    Magnesium.    Zinc.    Iron.

c Write a reactivity series for the metals in the pictures above.

Patterns of reactivity

Metals reacting with water and acid

The reactivity series when metals react with acids is almost exactly the same as when metals react with water.

Look at the table. It shows the reactivity series for metals with acids. Is it the same as your answer for question **c**?

Here is a reactivity series table showing more metals.

Reactivity series
potassium
calcium
magnesium
zinc
iron

Reactivity series
potassium
sodium
lithium
calcium
magnesium
zinc
iron
copper
silver
gold

d Name a metal beginning with 's' that is more reactive than zinc.

e Name a metal that is more reactive than zinc but less reactive than lithium.

QUESTIONS

Copy these sentences and write **true** or **false** next to each one:

Metals react with oxygen but not with acids.

Metals react with acids to produce hydrogen.

A salt is never produced when metals react with acids.

Gold is not a very reactive metal.

Potassium is a very reactive metal.

KEY POINTS

- Metals react with acids.
- The reactivity series of metals is the same with acid, with oxygen and with water.

Patterns of reactivity

F4 CAN METALS DISPLACE EACH OTHER?

What is displacement?

Displacement means to move from one place to another.

In science, displacement means that one chemical has pushed another one out of its compound and replaced it.

This is easier to understand if we think of an example.

We put zinc metal into iron sulphate. The zinc pushes the iron out of the way and replaces it. It makes zinc sulphate. Iron is also formed.

We say that the zinc has **displaced** the iron.

The pictures show what happens when we put zinc into iron sulphate solution. The colour changes.

The zinc is stronger or more reactive than the iron. So the zinc displaces the iron.

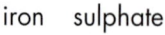

a Look at the reactivity series on page 57. Which is more reactive, zinc or iron?

Which metals displace other metals?

Imagine we did not have a reactivity series table. We want to know which is more reactive, iron or copper. We could find out by doing a little experiment.

First we place a piece of copper in iron sulphate solution.

We can see in the top photograph that there is no change.

Then we place a piece of iron in copper sulphate solution.

We can see in the second photograph that a reaction happens. Iron has displaced the copper.

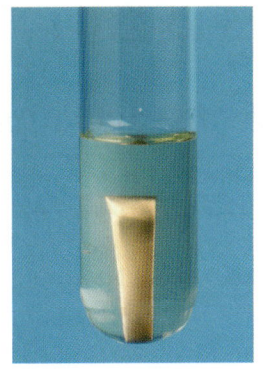

b Which is more reactive, iron or copper?

Look at the table on page 57 to see if you are right.

We can use experiments like this to find out how reactive other metals are. We can then put them in their correct order in the reactivity series.

Aluminium will displace zinc. But aluminium will not displace magnesium.

c Where should aluminium go in the reactivity series?

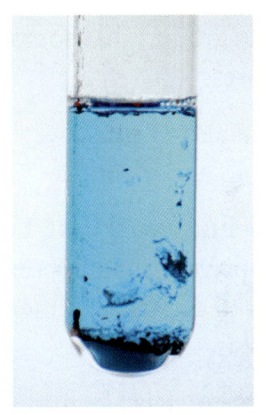

Copper in iron sulphate.

Iron in copper sulphate.

Some displacement reactions are very useful

Look at the picture. It shows aluminium displacing iron from iron oxide. The iron that is formed is molten. It is so hot that it can even weld railway lines together.

QUESTIONS

List the following metals in order of reactivity, most reactive first. Look back at previous pages to help you.

iron, gold, magnesium, silver, potassium, copper, lithium

KEY POINTS

- More reactive metals displace less reactive metals from their compounds.

F5 HOW IS REACTIVITY USEFUL?

How are metals found in nature?

Metals are found in the ground. But only metals like silver and gold can be found as pieces of metal.

Other metals, like aluminium, are more reactive. These are found as compounds. The reactivity series can help us understand why we find some metals in nature and others as compounds.

Rocks in the ground that contain metal compounds are called **ores**.

The first metals to be discovered were the unreactive ones like gold and silver.

Copper was discovered next. Even though it did not exist as copper metal, it was easy to get from its ore. All you had to do was heat the ore and the copper came out of it.

More reactive metals like iron were discovered next. You had to heat the ore with carbon to get the metal out of it.

The most reactive metals were difficult to get from their ores. This is why they have only been extracted from their ores in the last 200 years.

a Which metals were discovered first? Explain your answer.

Can we use the reactivity series?

The reactivity series helps us choose the best way of extracting a metal from its ore. Look at the reactivity series.

To get metals below carbon, like zinc and iron, you heat the ore with carbon.

But to get metals above carbon, like magnesium or calcium, you have to use large amounts of electricity. Carbon will not extract them from their ore.

b Name a metal that needs electricity to be extracted from its ore.

Gold nuggget.

Aluminium ore.

Reactivity series
potassium
sodium
lithium
calcium
magnesium
aluminium
carbon
zinc
iron
copper
silver
gold

Patterns of reactivity

How does the reactivity of a metal affect how we use it?

Gold would be an excellent metal to use for water pipes. It would never react with the water. Copper is nearly as good because it is not very reactive. It is much cheaper than gold.

c Why are water pipes not made of gold?

Silver is a good choice for making knives and forks. The silver will not react with the water or with dilute acids found in food.

d Why are knives and forks not made out of iron?

Jewellery is made out of metals like gold and silver. This is because they will not react with anything and will always stay shiny. But because the metals are very rare, they are very expensive.

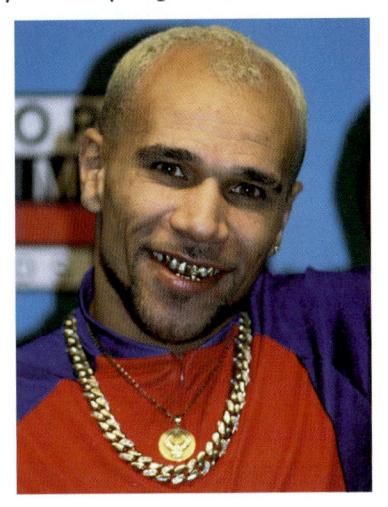

Copper water pipes.

e Why are gold and silver expensive?

QUESTIONS

Copy these sentences and fill in the spaces using the words below:

carbon   electricity

For metals more reactive than _____ , you extract them from their ores using _____ .

For metals less reactive than _____ , you extract them by heating them with carbon.

KEY POINTS

- If a metal is less reactive than carbon, we heat its ore with carbon to get the metal out.
- If a metal is more reactive than carbon, we have to use electricity to extract the metal.

G Environmental chemistry

G1 HOW ARE SOILS DIFFERENT?

What are the characteristics of soils?

Not all soils are the same.

Chalky soil is pale with white stones.

Sandy soil often has a yellowish colour.

Clay soil is usually brown.

Soil takes about a thousand years to make. It is made up from small bits of rock. The type of soil depends on what kind of rock the soil was made from.

Soil also contains the remains of dead plants and animals. This is called **organic material**.

a What do we call the dead remains of animal and plant material in the soil?

Some soils have large grains. They let water drain through easily.

Some soils have small grains. Water cannot drain easily through these soils.

What is the best soil for growing plants?

There is no such thing as a best soil. Different plants prefer different kinds of soils.

Some soils are acidic and others are alkaline. We can test the soil with a soil testing kit to see what the pH is.

A soil testing kit.

Look at the table. It shows what pH different plants prefer. If you know the pH of your soil, you can decide which plants would grow best in it.

Plant	pH the plant prefers
wheat	5.5 to 7.5
barley	6.5 to 7.8
oats	5.0 to 7.5
potatoes	4.8 to 6.5
strawberries	5.0 to 6.5
peaches	6.0 to 7.5
cranberries	4.2 to 5.0
broccoli	6.0 to 7.0

b What pH range do strawberries prefer?

c Which plant prefers a pH of 4.8 to 6.5?

Can we make a soil better for growing plants?

When farmers are deciding which crop to grow, they need to know the pH of their soil. Most soils in the UK have a pH of about 5. This means that if a farmer wants to grow barley, which needs a pH of 7, there are three choices:
1. Do not grow barley and choose a different crop like potatoes.
2. Accept that barley will not grow well.
3. Change the pH of the soil to pH 7.

The farmer can raise the pH by adding lime to the soil. The farmer has to know just how much lime to add to make the soil just right.

Spreading lime.

QUESTIONS

Copy these sentences and fill in the spaces using the words below:

    lime   pH   rocks   7

Soils are made from the remains of different _____. Farmers can measure the _____ of their soil with a soil testing kit. If the soil has too low a pH the farmer can add _____. Crops like barley prefer a pH of about _____.

KEY POINTS

- Soils are made from the weathered remains of different rocks.
- Different soils have different pHs.
- Farmers can raise the pH by adding lime.

Environmental chemistry

G2 HOW DO ROCKS CHANGE?

Do rocks look different as they get older?

As time passes, rocks change. They can change shape. They can change colour.

Look at the picture of the statue. It is made from rock. When it was made the features on the face were clear and easy to see.

a What has happened to the rock statue as time has passed?

What makes rocks change?

Rocks change because of **weathering**. Rain and temperature changes are two of the main things that change rocks.

Look at the pictures of the two monuments. They have been exposed to different kinds of weathering. As time has passed they have changed differently.

b The monument on the left is in London. The monument on the right is in Egypt. What kind of weather would each monument have?

Weathering is usually a slow process. We do not notice changes in the rocks from day to day.

There are two different ways that rocks can be weathered.

Chemical weathering

Rocks can be weathered by acidic rainwater. This is **chemical weathering**. Limestone in particular is weathered by rainwater.

Look at the picture. It shows how the rainwater has reacted with limestone, taking some of it away.

On page 44 you saw how acids react with limestone to form water, a salt and carbon dioxide.

c Where do you think the carbon dioxide from the limestone has gone?

Physical weathering

Changes in temperature cause **physical weathering**.

- Water gets into cracks in rocks. When the water freezes, it expands and makes the rock split.
- Even without water, the rock itself expands when it gets hot. It contracts when it gets cold. This can also cause the rock to split.
- Wind and water can rub rocks against each other. This also causes physical weathering.

What factors affect weathering?

Factors that affect weathering include:

- how hot or cold the weather is
- how wet or dry the weather is.

Look at the bar charts for rainfall in London and Egypt.

d Do the bar charts agree with your answer to question b?

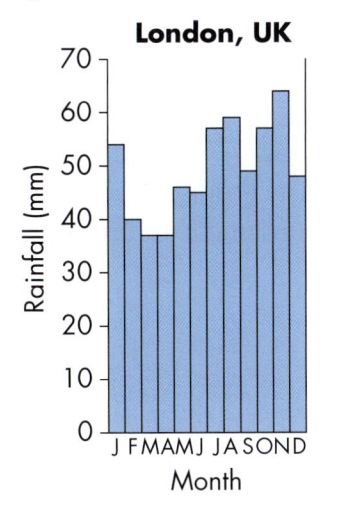

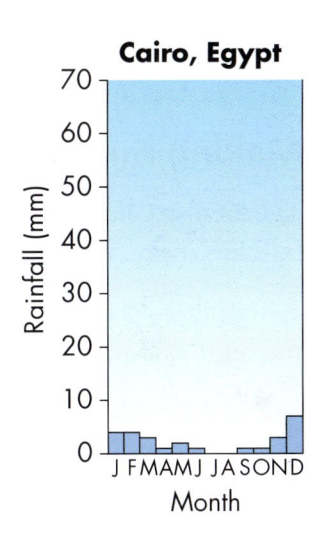

QUESTIONS

Copy these sentences and write **true** or **false** next to each one:

Acidic rainwater causes chemical weathering to rocks.

Physical weathering can be caused by changes in temperature.

Water freezing in cracks is an example of chemical weathering.

KEY POINTS

- Rocks change as they get older.
- Chemical and physical weathering can both change rocks.

Environmental chemistry

G3 WHAT CAUSES ACID RAIN?

How acidic is pure rainwater?

As rain falls from a cloud, it passes through the air. One of the gases in air is carbon dioxide. You may remember that plants need carbon dioxide for **photosynthesis**.

As the rain falls, some of the carbon dioxide in the air dissolves in the rainwater. This turns the rainwater into a weak acid called carbonic acid.

So rainwater is a weak acid.

> **a** What gas dissolves in rainwater to turn it into a weak acid?

The pH of pure water is pH 7. The pH of rainwater is pH 6. This tells us that rainwater is a weak acid.

Carbon dioxide makes rainwater a weak acid: pH 6. When you add universal indicator it turns yellow.

Making rainwater more acidic

The air also contains some waste products that humans make. We call these substances **pollutants**.

Two of these pollutants are sulphur dioxide and nitrogen oxides.

Sulphur dioxide reacts with water to form sulphuric acid.

Nitrogen oxides react with water to form nitric acid.

These are strong acids which make the rainwater much more acidic. We call this rainwater **acid rain**. It can have a pH between 2 and 5.

> **b** Which gases dissolve in rainwater to turn it into acid rain?
>
> **c** What is the pH of acid rain?

Sulphur dioxide makes rainwater a strong acid: pH 3. When you add universal indicator it turns red.

Environmental chemistry

Where does the acid come from?

Look at the diagram. Sulphur dioxide and nitrogen oxides come from many different places.

The bigger the arrow, the more gas is produced.

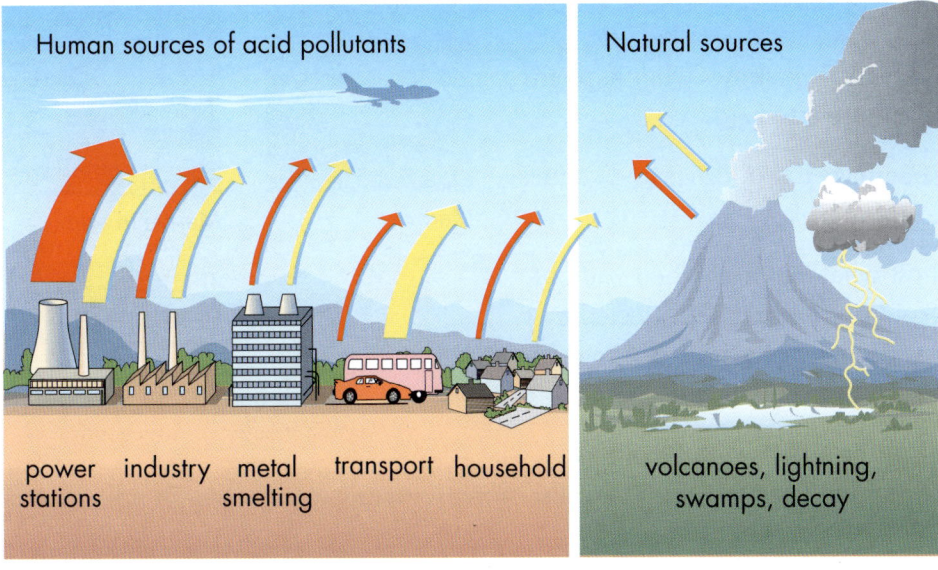

Human sources of acid pollutants: power stations, industry, metal smelting, transport, household

Natural sources: volcanoes, lightning, swamps, decay

↑ sulphur dioxide   ↑ nitrogen oxides

d Look at the picture. Where does most of the sulphur dioxide in the air come from?

e Name one natural source of sulphur dioxide pollution.

QUESTIONS

1 Copy these sentences and fill in the spaces using the words below:

   7   2 and 5   carbon dioxide

   Pure water has a pH of _____. When _____ dissolves in rainwater its pH is 6. Acid rain has a pH between _____.

2 Name two substances that cause rainwater to become acid rain.

3 How do these two substances get into the air?

KEY POINTS

- Carbon dioxide dissolves in rainwater to make it a weak acid.
- Sulphur dioxide and nitrogen oxides react with rainwater to turn it into acid rain.
- The pH of normal rainwater is pH 6. The pH of acid rain is between pH 2 and pH 5.

Environmental chemistry

G4 WHAT DOES ACID RAIN DO?

How does acid rain affect rocks and building materials?

Buildings are often made from rocks.

Some buildings and statues are made from limestone and marble.

Look at the right-hand picture. It shows what happens when you put rocks like these into acid.

Acid rain does a lot of damage to buildings and statues made from limestone and marble.

Marble.   Marble in acid.

The pictures below show what happens when you put sandstone into acid. Sand is not normally affected by acid. But sandstone has particles of sand stuck together by lime.

The acid reacts with the lime and the grains of sand just fall apart. So buildings made of sandstone are also affected by acid rain.

Sandstone.   Sandstone in acid.

a Why does acid rain break up sandstone?

What are the effects of acid rain on living things?

Acid rain affects plants more than animals. This is because animals can move out of the rain and take shelter.

Look at the picture. The trees have lost their leaves. They have been killed by acid rain.

b Why have the trees in the picture died?

It usually takes many months or years for acid rain to have this effect on trees.

Acid rain can also affect lakes. The lake gradually becomes more acidic. This kills plants in the lake. The fish then die from lack of food and oxygen.

Look at the picture. The lake looks crystal clear. All life has been killed, just leaving clear water behind. The lake is dead.

How can we reduce acid rain?

We can reduce acid rain by putting less pollutants into the environment.

Nitrogen oxides are present in car exhaust fumes. We reduce this pollution by fitting cars with **catalytic converters**. A catalytic converter turns the polluting gases into harmless nitrogen and water.

Some power stations burn coal. They release large amounts of sulphur dioxide into the air. They can fit equipment that removes the sulphur dioxide from the gases that go up the chimney.

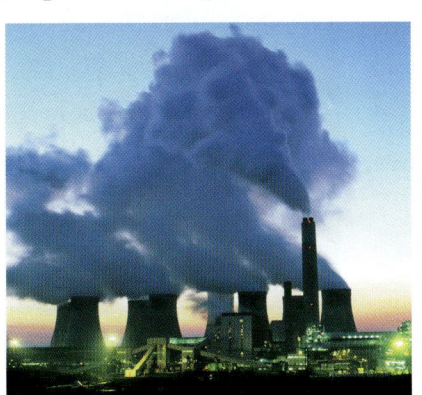

c Name two ways that we can reduce the pollutants that cause acid rain.

QUESTIONS

Copy these sentences and fill in the spaces using the words below:

acid   catalytic   limestone   sulphur

Acid rain can damage buildings made of _____ . We can reduce the amount of acid rain by fitting _____ converters onto car exhausts. Power stations release lots of _____ dioxide that also causes _____ rain.

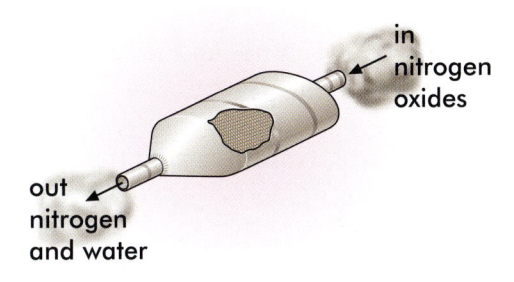

KEY POINTS

- Acid rain can damage buildings made of limestone or marble.
- We can reduce acid rain by using catalytic converters on car exhausts.
- We can reduce acid rain by removing sulphur dioxide from the gases released from power stations.

Environmental chemistry

G5 WHAT'S HAPPENING TO THE ENVIRONMENT?

How is pollution monitored today?

It is easy to find out about pollution levels in the past. We can:

- look at old photographs of buildings and compare them to how the buildings look now
- look at past medical records to see how pollution has affected people's health
- look at newspapers, books and diaries.

a How can we find out how pollution affected people in the past?

Today scientists **monitor** pollution levels. This means they measure and keep track of the levels of pollutants in the air.

One way scientists collect this information is by using satellites. Satellites measure the amount of pollution in the atmosphere, and what this is doing to our weather.

Scientists also get information from organisms such as lichens. These grow on trees, rocks and buildings.

The picture below shows one kind of lichen. Different lichens can survive in different levels of pollution. Some lichens can grow in polluted air. Others can only grow in pure air. By looking at which lichens are growing, scientists can measure the levels of pollution.

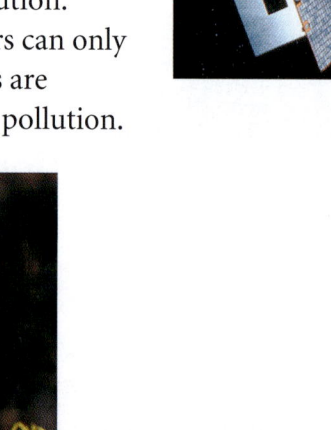

b Name two ways that scientists can monitor levels of pollution.

Environmental chemistry

The greenhouse effect

The Sun warms the Earth. Some heat from the Earth is lost into space, but some of it is reflected back to the Earth by gases in our atmosphere. We call this the **greenhouse effect**.

Carbon dioxide in the atmosphere reflects heat back to the surface of the Earth. Carbon dioxide is acting just like glass in a greenhouse. It traps the heat in, making the Earth warmer.

If we have too much carbon dioxide in the atmosphere, the Earth could warm up too much. We call this danger **global warming**.

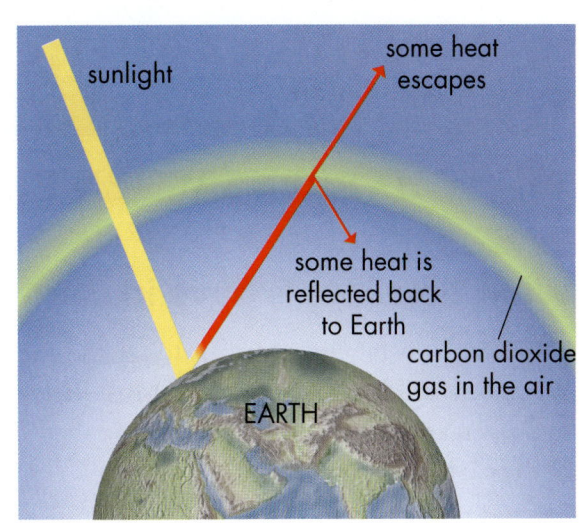

The greenhouse effect.

Is global warming happening?

Records show that the Earth is warming up. This may be because we are putting more and more carbon dioxide into the atmosphere. Or this warming may be a natural change.

One thing is sure. If the planet warms up too much, oceans will expand, ice at the Poles will melt and sea levels will rise. This will cause flooding in some parts of the world. Weather patterns will also change.

What can we do to reduce global warming?

Scientists and world leaders have met to discuss the problem of global warming. Scientists are getting worried that we should act before it is too late. All the countries need to put less carbon dioxide into the atmosphere. Getting countries to agree to this is not as easy as you might think.

QUESTIONS

Carbon dioxide is produced by cars, industry and power stations.

Make a list of reasons why some countries might not want to reduce the amount of carbon dioxide that they release into the atmosphere.

KEY POINTS

- Scientists monitor levels of pollutants very accurately.
- Rising levels of carbon dioxide may lead to global warming.

Environmental chemistry

H Using chemistry

H1 WHAT HAPPENS WHEN FUELS BURN?

What do all fuels have in common?

A **fuel** is a substance that burns to release energy. It can be a solid, a liquid or a gas. Most fuels contain hydrogen and carbon. These fuels are called **hydrocarbons**.

Petrol burning.

What is made when a hydrocarbon fuel burns?

For a fuel to burn it needs oxygen. The air contains oxygen. This is why fuels will burn in air.

When a hydrocarbon fuel reacts with oxygen, it always produces water and carbon dioxide.

hydrocarbon fuel + oxygen ⟶ water vapour + carbon dioxide

One of the fuels we use is a gas called methane. The gas for a gas cooker or Bunsen burner is methane.

methane + oxygen ⟶ water vapour + carbon dioxide

We usually think of water as putting out fires, so it seems strange to think that a burning fuel makes water!

You can see that burning methane makes water when you use a Bunsen burner. Look at the picture. The outside of the beaker of cold water has steamed up. Water vapour from the Bunsen burner flame has condensed on the cold beaker.

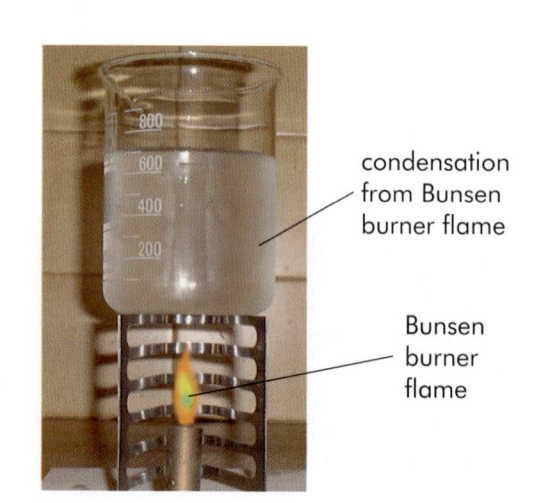

condensation from Bunsen burner flame

Bunsen burner flame

a What two things are produced when methane burns in air?

What happens when there is not enough oxygen?

Sometimes when we burn fuels there is not enough oxygen. This can happen in our homes.

If a gas heater has a blocked flue, not enough oxygen gets to the burning gas. When this happens the fuel burns to produce carbon monoxide.

methane + not enough oxygen ⟶ water vapour + carbon monoxide

Carbon monoxide is a very dangerous gas. It is very poisonous. We cannot see it, smell it or taste it so we cannot tell when it is produced.

This is why it is very important to look after gas heaters and have them serviced. Every year people die of carbon monoxide poisoning from faulty gas heaters.

b What is produced when methane burns without enough oxygen?

c Explain why it is dangerous.

What is a good fuel?

Look at the table. The more questions you can answer 'yes' to, the better the fuel.

d Answer as many of the questions as you can about coal.

1. Is a lot of heat produced?
2. Is the fuel easy to light?
3. Does the fuel burn slowly?
4. Does the fuel keep burning?
5. Is the fuel easily available?
6. Is the fuel easy to store?
7. Is the fuel easy to transport?
8. Is little or no smoke produced?
9. Is little or no ash left behind?
10. Is the fuel safe?
11. Is the fuel cheap?

We can get heat energy from a chemical reaction

KEY POINTS

- Most fuels contain hydrogen and carbon (they are hydrocarbons).
- Hydrocarbons burn to produce water and carbon dioxide.

QUESTIONS

1. What is a fuel?
2. What two elements are found in hydrocarbon fuels?
3. What is produced when hydrocarbons burn?

H2 DO OTHER CHEMICAL REACTIONS SUPPLY ENERGY?

Can chemical reactions supply energy?

Chemical reactions can release energy. The energy comes in many different forms.

We get heat and light from burning wood.

We get electricity from a battery.

We get explosions from dynamite.

We get movement from a car engine.

a What type of energy do we get from a rocket?

In Unit F you looked at displacement reactions.

You may have noticed that when you put magnesium into iron sulphate solution, the test tube got warm. The further apart the metals are in the reactivity series, the warmer the test tube gets. We can get heat energy from displacement reactions.

Can we make electrical energy?

Look at the picture. If you put two different metals into a liquid that conducts electricity, the bulb lights. Liquids that conduct electricity are called **electrolytes**. The reaction is producing electricity to make the light bulb glow.

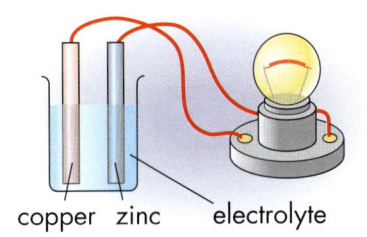

Some pairs of metals will make the bulb glow brighter. The further apart the metals are in the reactivity series, the brighter the bulb will be.

b Look back at page 60. Which pair will give a brighter bulb, copper and magnesium, or copper and iron?

Other uses of energy from chemicals

Most of the electricity we use is produced in power stations. It is made by burning fossil fuels like coal, oil and gas.

Another way to produce electrical energy is to use a **fuel cell**.

In a fuel cell, a chemical reaction generates electricity without burning. Fuel cells are like batteries, but much smaller and lighter. They are used on the Space Shuttle.

Some cars have fuel cells instead of burning petrol.

QUESTIONS

Copy these sentences and fill in the spaces using the words below:

electrical   heat   light   metals

Burning wood releases _____ and _____ energy. A car battery releases _____ energy. Electrical energy is also released when you put two different _____ in an electrolyte.

KEY POINTS

- Chemical reactions release different kinds of energy.

H3 WHAT NEW MATERIALS CAN WE MAKE FROM CHEMICALS?

How many different materials can we produce?

We produce millions of different materials. No one has ever been able to count them. New materials are being made every day.

Over two million different materials are made from crude oil. This is why oil is so important to us. Plastics are just one example.

Many more materials are produced by living things in nature. Flour from wheat is just one example.

ⓐ Name a material that can be made from oil and a material that can be made by a living organism.

Plants are very good at making materials. They make glucose by photosynthesis. Then they turn the glucose into many different materials, such as proteins and fats.

ⓑ Can you think of any other materials that plants make?

Animals eat the plants. They turn the materials into even more different materials.

ⓒ Can you think of any other material that animals make? Think about when you cut your hair or your fingernails.

76 Using chemistry

How is a new chemical developed?

These steps show how a new chemical for farming, such as a weedkiller, is developed.

1. First thousands of chemicals are made and tested to see if they kill weeds.

2. Chemicals that do kill weeds are chosen, and permission is given to test them further.

3. A few promising chemicals are tested first in the lab, then in greenhouses and outside on farms. Scientists measure their effect on the environment.

4. The results of these tests are checked to see if the chemicals are dangerous to people or the environment.

5. They then find out whether farmers will want to buy the new weedkiller if it is produced.

6. After more tests, permission is given to sell the new product.

7. The new weedkiller is sold to farmers who use it on their farms.

QUESTIONS

Copy these sentences and write **true** or **false** next to each one:

Crude oil can only be used to make petrol.
New materials are being discovered every day.
Plants and animals make many different kinds of material.

KEY POINTS

- There are many millions of different materials.
- New materials are being made every day.

H4 WHAT HAPPENS TO ATOMS IN A CHEMICAL REACTION?

How are atoms rearranged?

In a chemical reaction, the atoms become rearranged. This makes new substances. But the new substances are made from exactly the same atoms that we started with.

New atoms are never made and old atoms are never destroyed during a chemical reaction.

In Unit F4 we looked at iron in copper sulphate solution. We saw how the iron displaced the copper to make iron sulphate and copper.

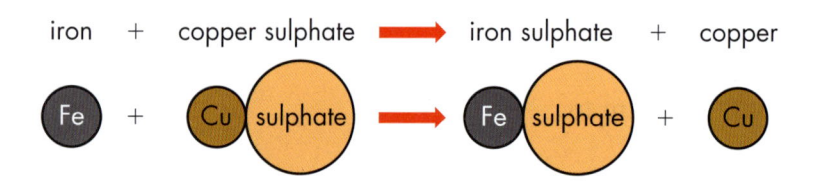

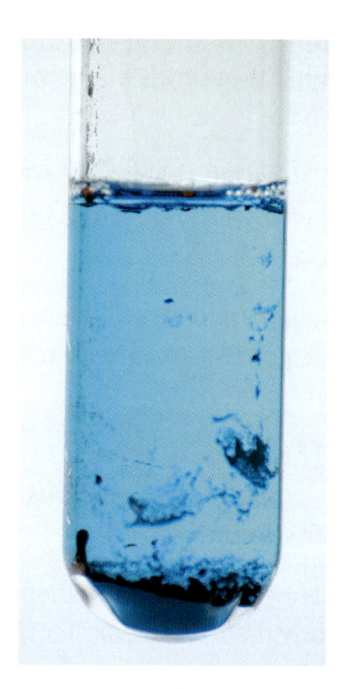

iron + copper sulphate → iron sulphate + copper

Fe + Cu sulphate → Fe sulphate + Cu

a Look at the equation above.
  i   How many iron atoms are on the left-hand side of the arrow?
  ii How many iron atoms are on the right-hand side of the arrow?
  iii What do you notice about these two numbers?

b Answer the same questions for copper. What do you notice?

For each reaction, the number of atoms on the left is always the same as the number of atoms on the right.

How much is used up?

Look at the picture. It shows the mass of the substances used and the mass of the new substances that are produced in this reaction.

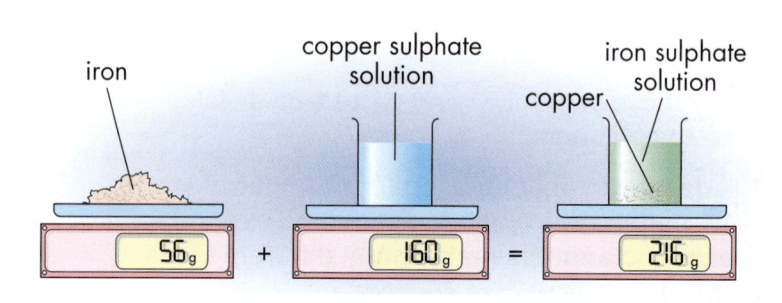

iron 56 g + copper sulphate solution 160 g = copper, iron sulphate solution 216 g

Using chemistry

c Add together the mass of the iron powder and the mass of the copper sulphate solution. Compare your answer with the mass of the copper and iron sulphate solution. What do you notice?

The theory of conservation of mass

In any reaction, we always end up with what we started with. We just rearrange the atoms.

There are never any exceptions to this rule. Scientists call this rule the **theory of conservation of mass**.

> Mass is neither created nor destroyed in a chemical reaction.

This means the amount of stuff you put into a chemical reaction is always *exactly* the same as the amount you get out.

This theory is also true for dissolving things.

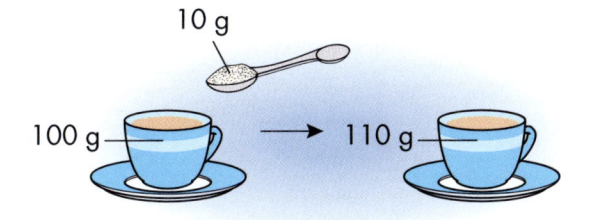

You start with 100 g of tea. You add 10 g of sugar. Then you have 110 g of sugary tea. The total mass has not changed, even though you cannot see the sugar any more.

QUESTIONS

Copy these sentences choosing only the correct words:

During a chemical reaction the atoms **are / are not** rearranged.

During a chemical reaction, mass **is / is not** created.

If you stir 20 g of sugar into 100 g of tea, the mass of the tea will be **20 g / 100 g / 120 g**.

KEY POINTS

- During a chemical reaction the atoms are rearranged.
- During a chemical reaction mass is neither created nor destroyed.

H5 PROVING THE THEORY OF CONSERVATION OF MASS

Evidence for the theory of conservation of mass

Scientists do not believe theories unless there is plenty of evidence for them. Here is more evidence to show that the theory of conservation of mass in correct.

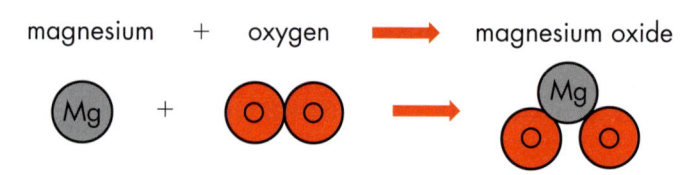

magnesium + oxygen → magnesium oxide

Magnesium burns in air to make magnesium oxide.

Look at the pictures. They show an experiment to burn magnesium in air.

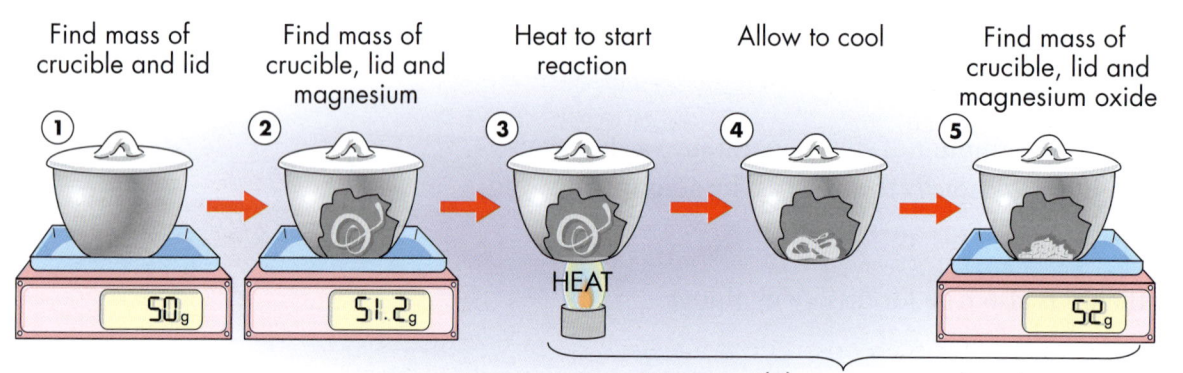

1. Find mass of crucible and lid — 50 g
2. Find mass of crucible, lid and magnesium — 51.2 g
3. Heat to start reaction
4. Allow to cool
5. Find mass of crucible, lid and magnesium oxide — 52 g

Repeat until the mass stops changing

This is quite a tricky experiment to do. When magnesium burns, you sometimes see some smoke blowing away. The smoke is really magnesium oxide.

To make the experiment accurate, we must not lose any magnesium oxide as smoke. This is why we burn the magnesium in a crucible with a lid on. It keeps in all of the smoke.

If you lift the lid to let in some air, you must be careful not to let any smoke out.

a The magnesium weighed 50 g at the start of the experiment.
The magnesium oxide weighed 52 g at the end of the experiment.
How much did the oxygen weigh that combined with the magnesium?

This tells us that 0.8 g of oxygen has combined with 1.2 g of magnesium. The reaction makes 2 g of magnesium oxide, so the theory is right again.

How a scientist called Lavoisier proved the theory

H5

Antoine Lavoisier was a French scientist who lived in the 1700s. He was one of the first people to prove the theory of conservation of mass.

In 1775 he carried out a famous experiment that took twelve days and nights to complete.

1. Lavoisier heated mercury in a flask of air. The mercury reacted with oxygen to form mercury oxide.

2. The reaction took the oxygen from the air in the jar. The volume of air got less and the mercury rose in the jar.

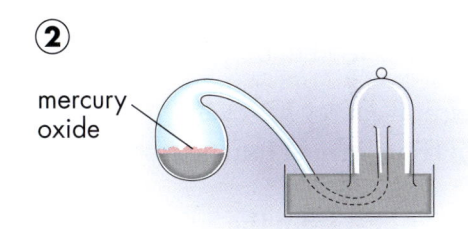

3. He then placed the mercury oxide in a clean flask and heated it very strongly. It gave off oxygen. He collected this in a jar full of mercury. The volume of oxygen produced was exactly the same as the volume of oxygen used in step **2**.

   This gives more evidence that things aren't created or destroyed during chemical reactions, they are just rearranged. The theory wins again.

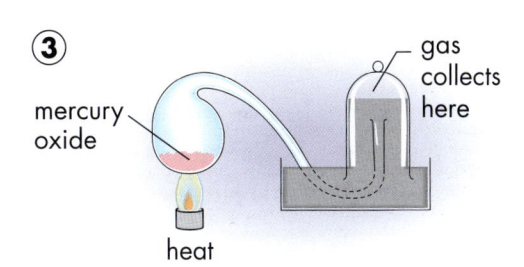

QUESTIONS

Copy these sentences and fill in the spaces using the words below:

> mercury   conservation   oxygen
> experiments   Lavoisier   oxide

We can prove the theory of _____ of mass by doing _____. A scientist called _____ was one of the first people to prove the theory. He heated _____ and air to make mercury _____. When he heated the mercury oxide it turned back into mercury and _____.

KEY POINTS

- We can do experiments to prove the theory of conservation of mass.
- Lavoisier was one of the first scientists to prove the theory in 1775.

Using chemistry

1 Energy and electricity

1.1 HOW IS ENERGY USEFUL FOR DOING THINGS?

Transfers and transformations

When you put a spoon in a hot drink, the spoon gets hot. Heat energy has moved. It has **transferred** from the hot tea to the cold spoon.

Fuels such as gas have energy stored in them. The energy is stored as **chemical energy**. When we burn gas, the chemical energy in the gas is released as heat. The heat is used to boil the water in the saucepan.

Chemical energy has changed into heat energy. It has been **transformed** into heat energy.

a The heat from the boiling water makes the saucepan handle hot. Is the energy being transferred or transformed?

Energy is never lost or created. It is always transferred or transformed. For anything to happen, energy must be transferred or transformed.

For the car to move, chemical energy in the fuel is transformed to heat energy and then movement energy in the engine. This is transferred to movement energy in the wheels.

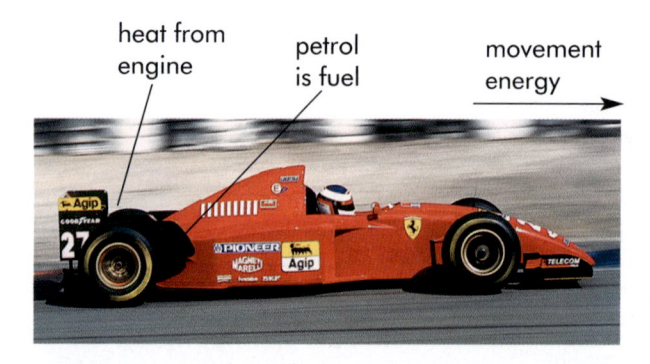

heat from engine   petrol is fuel   movement energy →

To make electricity, movement energy of the wind is transferred to movement energy of the windmills. This is transformed to electrical energy.

How can we store energy?

Energy can be stored in all sorts of ways:

- in the spring of a wind-up clock 
- as chemical energy in a cell 
- in a weight that has been lifted up high.

b In what ways can energy be stored?

Why is electrical energy useful?

Imagine what life would be like without electricity. There would be no television, computers or mobile phones. Life would be very difficult without electricity. Electricity is so useful to us because:

1. It is easy to transfer from place to place along power lines.
2. It leaves no waste substances when we use it.
3. It is easily transformed into other useful forms of energy.

c Why is electrical energy so useful to us?

QUESTIONS

Copy these sentences and fill in the spaces using the words below:

> transferred   transformed

When energy is changed from electricity into light we say the energy has been _____. When heat energy moves along a metal saucepan handle we say the energy has been _____.

KEY POINTS

- Energy can be transferred from one place to another.
- Energy can be transformed from one type to another.

Energy and electricity

12 HOW DOES ELECTRICITY TRANSFER ENERGY?

How is energy transferred in an electrical circuit?

Electrical energy is transferred round a circuit. We call this flow of electricity an electric current.

Useful things to remember

Adding more cells makes more current flow.

current flows, bulb lit

more cells
more current flows, brighter bulb

Adding more bulbs in series reduces the current.

Current is not used up in a circuit. It just carries energy from the cell to the bulb.

more bulbs
less current flows, bulbs dimmer

a What happens to the current if we add more cells?

b What happens to the current if we add more bulbs in series?

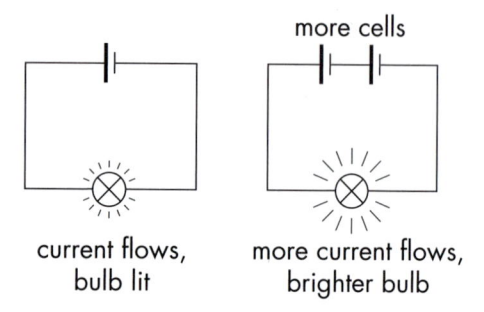

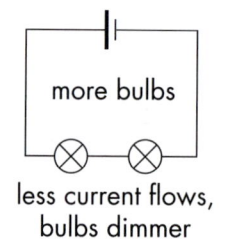

Where does the energy in a cell come from?

Cells contain chemicals. When the chemicals react together, chemical energy is transformed into electrical energy.

There is a chemical paste inside a cell. The outside shell is made of zinc. The paste and the zinc react together.

As they react, the zinc gradually gets thinner and thinner. Eventually it gets so thin the cell will leak. This is why you should never leave cells inside torches for too long.

chemical paste
carbon rod (positive)
zinc shell (negative)

c Why should you not leave a cell inside a torch for a long time?

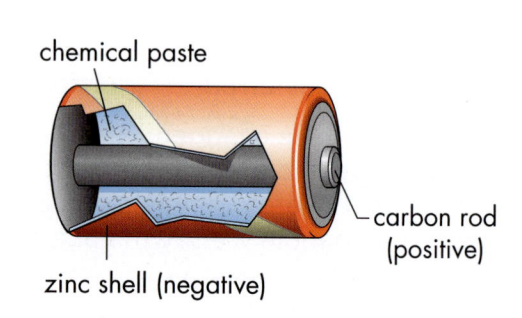

How much push?

Cells push electric current around a circuit.

We call this push the **voltage**. We can measure the voltage using a voltmeter. Look at the picture.

d How many volts is the cell pushing with?

If we put two cells together, we get twice the push.

The larger voltage makes a larger current flow. This makes the bulb glow brighter.

High voltages are dangerous

The voltage of the electrical supply that we use in our homes is 240 volts. This means that it can push much more current through our bodies. This makes it very dangerous. Power lines carry current at even higher voltages and are very dangerous indeed.

Lightning also has a very high voltage. This is why buildings such as churches have lightning conductors. They conduct the electric current to the ground and prevent the building from being damaged.

QUESTIONS

Copy and complete this crossword.

1 **down**   Electric _____ is a flow of electricity.
2 **across** Current flows around this.
3 **across** An extra cell makes a bulb glow _____.
4 **across** This is a measure of how much a cell pushes.

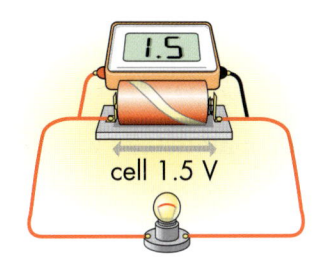

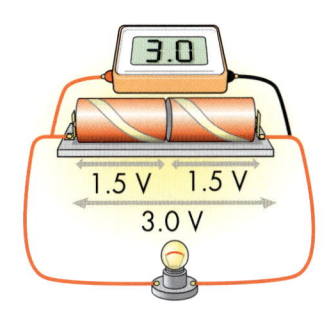

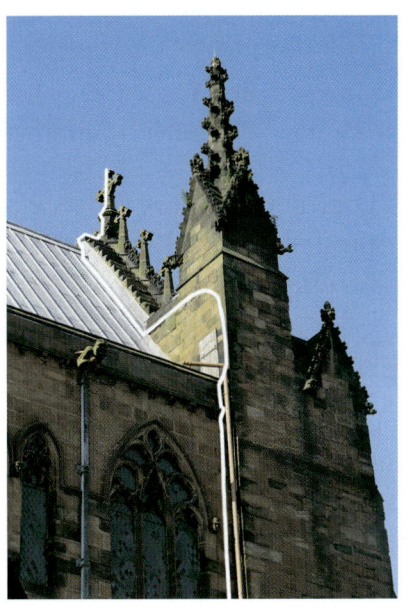

The white line on this photograph is a lightning conductor.

KEY POINTS

- Electric current is a flow of electricity around a circuit.
- Cells push the electric current round the circuit.
- Voltage is a measure of how hard the cells push.

13 MODELS OF ELECTRICITY

What is a model?

In science, a **model** is a way of trying to understand something that is not easy to understand. We cannot see electricity. But we can use models to help us understand how electric current flows around a circuit.

Marble model

- The moving marbles represent the current flowing around the circuit.
- The paddle wheel represents the bulb. The faster it turns, the brighter the bulb.
- The hand turning the handle represents the cell. The harder the hand pushes the handle, the greater the voltage.
- As the person gets tired, they turn the handle more slowly. The cell is running down.

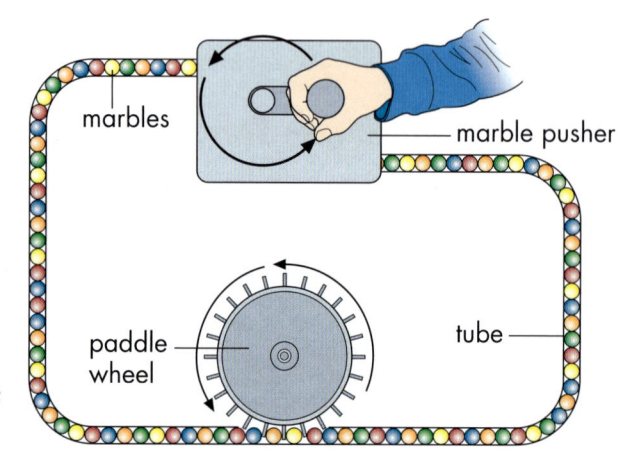

a Look at the picture above. What will happen to the paddle wheel as soon as the hand starts turning the handle?

Gerbil model

Look at the picture below. The clockwork gerbils get wound up at the winding station. The gerbils then go round the track. On the way they lose the energy in the clockwork spring to climb hills. By the time they return to the winding station they are almost run down.

- As the gerbils go round the track and climb hills, they lose energy.
- When they return to the winding station they are wound up again and given more energy.

b Does the winding station in this model represent a bulb or a cell?

c What does the Gerbil Winding Station give to the gerbils?

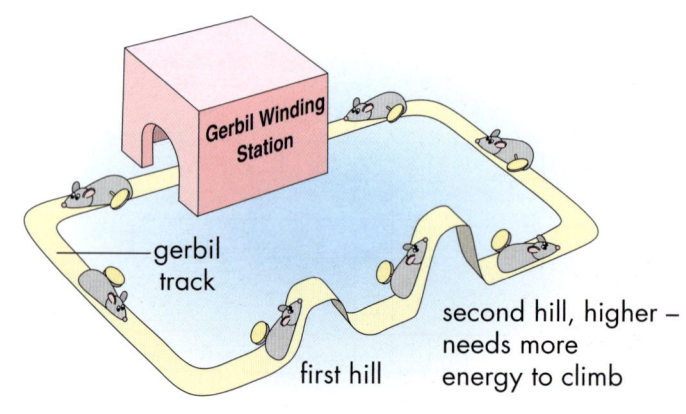

Energy and electricity

How can the marble model explain voltage?

Look at the picture. The model now has two people turning two handles. This is like putting an extra cell in the circuit. We now have twice the push and the paddle wheel turns twice as fast. In other words we have doubled the voltage.

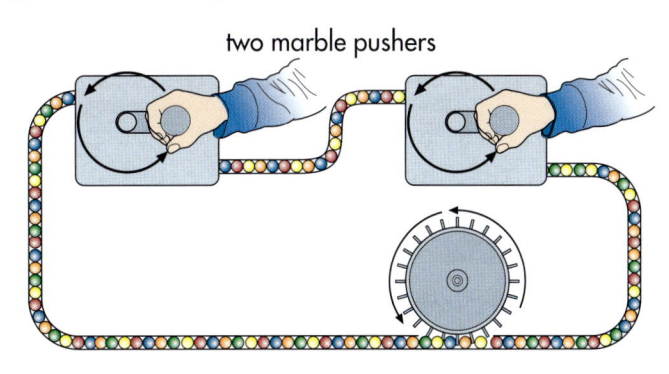

two marble pushers

How can the marble model explain current?

Look at the picture. If we add a second paddle wheel to the circuit it is more difficult for the person turning the handle. The flow of marbles is less. This is like putting an extra bulb in the circuit. Because the current is less, the bulbs are dimmer.

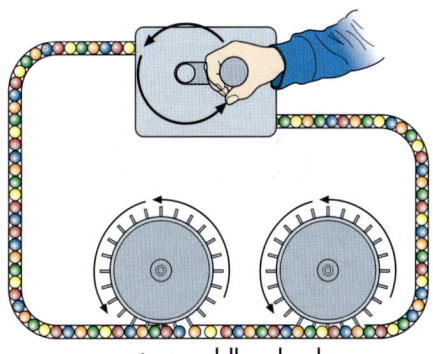

extra paddle wheel

How good are our models?

Models help us to understand something that is quite complicated. But no model is perfect. Some models explain some things better than others.

- The marble model is better for explaining how current flows round a circuit.
- The gerbil model is better for explaining how energy is transferred round the circuit.

QUESTIONS

Copy these sentences and fill in the spaces using the words below:

current   energy

The marble model helps us to understand how _____ flows round a circuit. The gerbil model helps us to understand how _____ is transferred round a circuit.

KEY POINTS

- Models help us to understand things that are complicated.

Energy and electricity

14 HOW DO WE USE ELECTRICITY?

How much energy do you use?

We use electricity in our homes. Electric cables carry **mains electricity** into our homes. The current transfers energy to wherever we want to use it in the house. The mains supply is at 240 volts. This means it can supply much more energy than a 1.5 volt cell used in a torch.

Diane decided to make a list of all the electrical devices that she used in one day. She timed how long she used them for. She also found out how much energy each one used in one hour. She wrote all this information in a table.

Device	Time used for in hours	Energy transferred per hour in kJ	Total energy transformed in kJ
water heater (bath)	1	11 160	11 160
light bulb	7	360	2520
kettle	0.1	10 800	1080
television	5	612	3060

a Look at the table. Which device used the most energy per hour?

Look at the picture. It shows different ways that electrical devices transform energy in our homes.

b Which device transforms electrical energy into light energy?

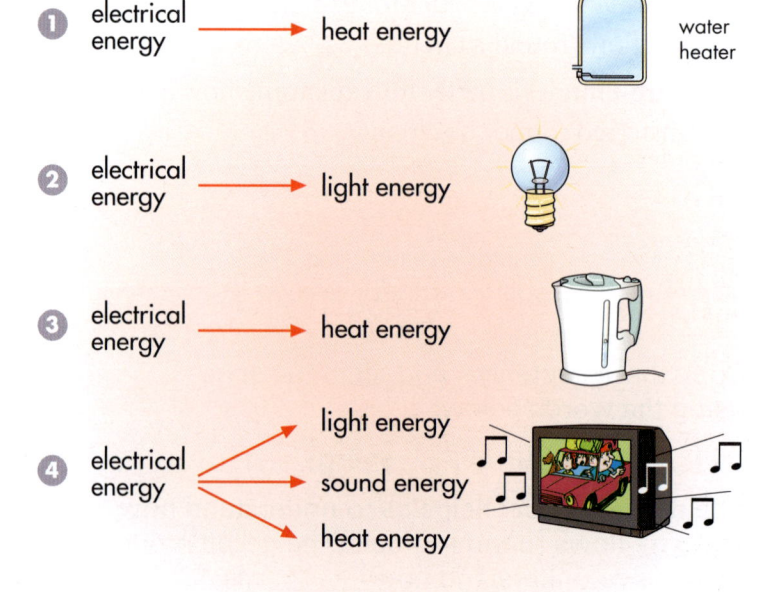

1. electrical energy ⟶ heat energy — water heater
2. electrical energy ⟶ light energy
3. electrical energy ⟶ heat energy
4. electrical energy ⟶ light energy, sound energy, heat energy

88 Energy and electricity

How can you use less electrical energy?

We need to use less energy. The more energy we use, the more pollution we make. Using less energy means we are doing less damage to the environment. It also saves us money.

A few simple changes to the way we live would make a big difference to the amount of energy that we use.

- Don't fill the kettle. Just put as much water in as you need.
- When you are cold, don't turn the heating up. Just put on an extra jumper.
- Shut the door! If you leave the door open, the heat will escape. You are spending money to heat up the garden.
- Use energy-efficient light bulbs. They turn more of the energy into useful light. This means they cost much less to run.
- Switch off the lights when you are not in the room.
- Don't leave TVs and video recorders on 'standby'. They only use a small amount of electricity but they are on for 24 hours a day. This soon adds up to a lot of electricity.
- Take a shower instead of a bath. It uses a lot less hot water.
- Insulate the house. Loft insulation, draught excluders and cavity wall insulation reduce a lot of heat loss. Most houses have little gaps around windows and doors. If you added them all together, it is like leaving a window open, all the time.

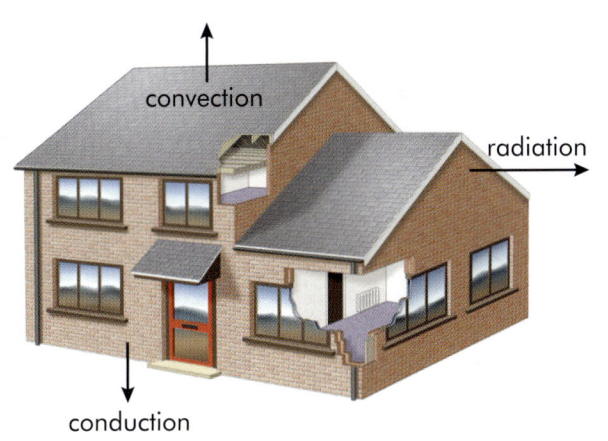

QUESTIONS

Look at the points listed on this page.

Make a list of all the things you could do in your own home to reduce the amount of electricity that your family uses.

KEY POINTS

- Electrical devices transform electrical energy into other kinds of energy.
- We can reduce the amount of electricity that we use.

15 WHERE DO WE GET ELECTRICITY FROM?

How does a dynamo work?

A dynamo on a bicycle makes electricity to light the lights. The dynamo is called a **generator**.

The bicycle wheel turns the dynamo. The dynamo then transforms this movement energy into electrical energy.

The faster you pedal, the more electricity you make. This is why the lights get brighter when you pedal faster.

How does a power station work?

In a power station, electricity is made in a similar way to the dynamo.

The generator is turned by steam instead of a moving bicycle wheel. The steam is made by heating water to boil it. The steam turns big fan blades called a **turbine**. The turbine then turns the generator. This transforms the movement energy into electrical energy.

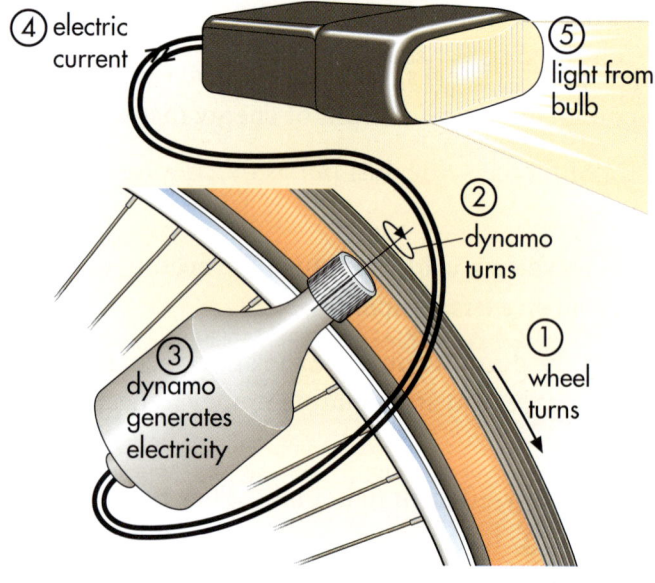

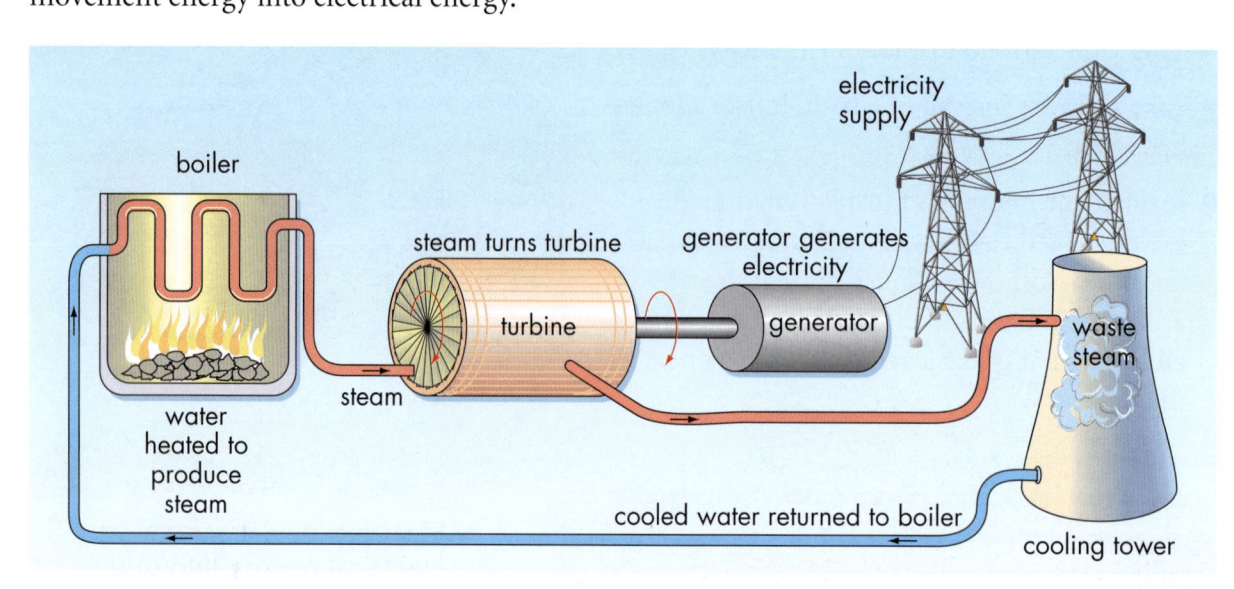

a What makes the turbine move in a power station?

b Which part of a power station is like the dynamo on your bicycle?

Energy and electricity

What are the problems of generating electricity?

- We use more energy during the day than at night. Power stations work best if they are used all the time without stopping at night.
- Electrical energy cannot be stored. Power stations generate electricity as we use it.
- Coal-fired power stations cause pollution when they burn the coal.
- Most power stations use coal and oil, which cannot be replaced.
- We need to use less electricity in order to save fossil fuels and reduce pollution.

C Why do we need to use less electricity?

How else can we generate electricity?

Another way to save fossil fuels and reduce pollution is to find another way of generating electricity. Here are some ways that do not burn fuel.

① Hydroelectric energy. Look at the power station in the picture. Water falling from the upper lake turns the turbines and generates electricity. At night when there is spare electricity, water from the lower lake is pumped back up to the top lake. Then it can be used in the daytime when more electricity is needed.

② Wave energy. The waves make floats bob up and down. This movement can be used to generate electricity.

③ Wind energy. The wind turns large windmills. These turn a generator to make electricity.

QUESTIONS

List three ways of generating electricity that do not produce pollution and do not use up fossil fuels.

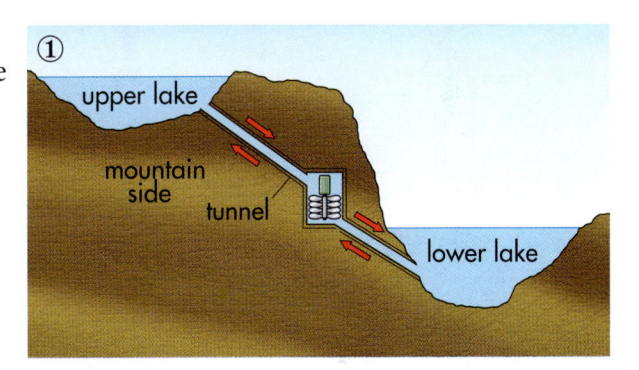

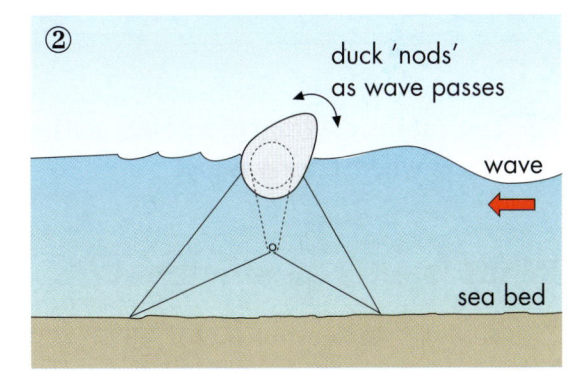

KEY POINTS

- Most power stations use fossil fuels and cause pollution.
- Alternative sources of energy do not use fossil fuels or cause pollution.

16 WHY IS ENERGY WASTED?

What type of energy is wasted?

When power stations burn fuel to generate electricity, they produce a lot of waste heat energy. This heat energy spreads out into the air. All of this heat energy is lost and we can no longer use it.

Look at the picture. It shows you how heat energy is lost into the air instead of being used to generate electricity.

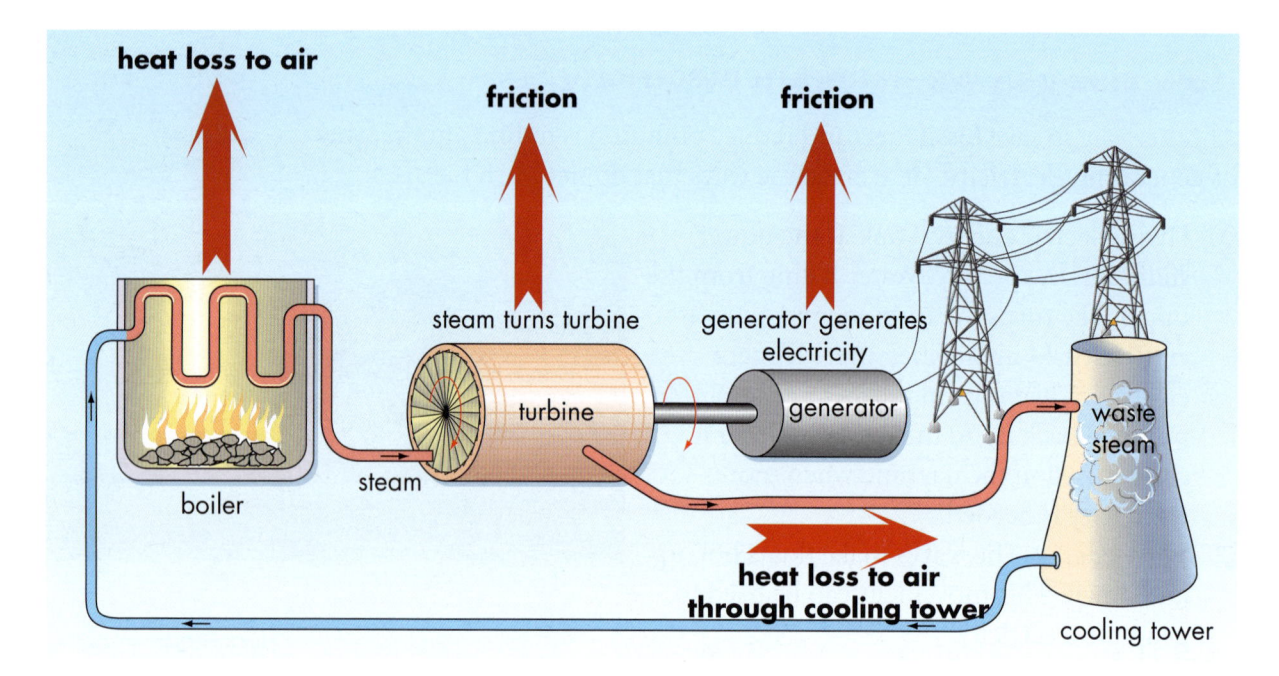

a Look at the diagram of a power station. List three places where energy is lost.

What is energy efficiency?

We can measure how much heat energy is produced by burning the fuel. Then we can work out how much of this energy gets transformed into electricity. This tells us how **efficient** a power station is.

Most power stations transform about 33% of the energy in the fuel to electricity. The other 67% gets transformed into heat energy and is lost. This tells us that power stations are not very efficient.

b How efficient is a power station?

How efficient are electrical devices?

Some devices such as an LED (Light Emitting Diode) are very efficient. They transform 99% of the electrical energy into light.

Other devices are less efficient. A light bulb transforms 90% of the electrical energy into wasted heat.

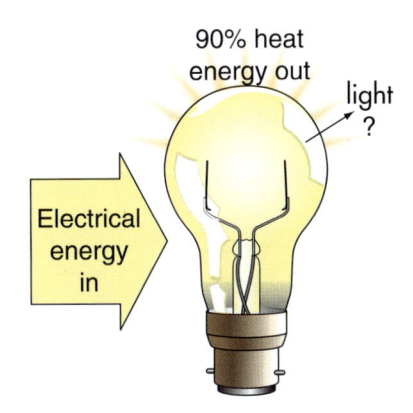

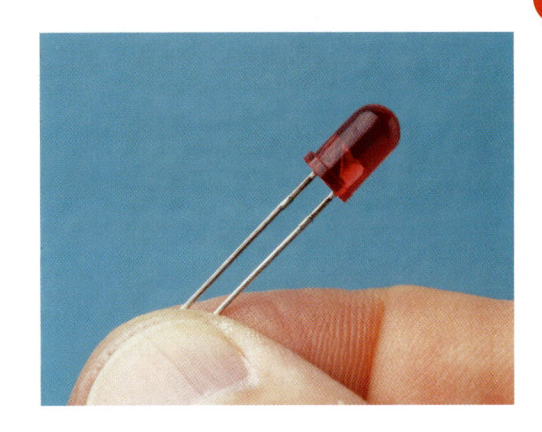

c How much of the electrical energy does a light bulb transform into useful light?

What is conservation of energy?

We know that many energy transformations produce wasted heat. Even though the heat is wasted, it is still there. It hasn't gone, but we cannot use it.

Whenever energy is transformed from one form to another, it still exists. We cannot make energy. We cannot destroy energy. We can only transform the energy from one form to another. This idea is called the **conservation of energy**.

QUESTIONS

1 Explain why an ordinary bulb is inefficient.
2 Explain why an LED is very efficient.

KEY POINTS

- When energy is transformed, some of it is lost as heat energy.
- Energy is not destroyed when it is transformed from one form to another.

J Gravity and space

J1 WHAT IS GRAVITY?

Mass and weight

Mass is the amount of material or 'stuff' there is in an object. We measure mass in **kilograms** (kg).

The kilogram mass in the picture will have the same mass no matter where we put it. Even in space it will still have a mass of 1 kg. Mass always stays the same.

Weight is a force. The weight of an object is how much the Earth pulls it downwards. It tells us how heavy the object is. We measure weight in units called **newtons** (N).

Weight does not always stay the same. If we put the 1 kg mass in space it will have no weight at all. But it will still be the same 1 kg mass.

On Earth a mass of 1 kg has a weight of 10 N.

a What will be the weight of a 1 kg mass in space?

Why do things fall?

If you jump from a tall building you fall downwards. You are really falling towards the centre of the Earth, but you stop when you hit the ground. Even people in Australia, which is on the opposite side of the planet, fall towards the centre of the Earth.

b In which direction do people in Africa fall?

The force that pulls us towards the centre of the Earth is called **gravity**.

c What is the name of the force that pulls us towards the centre of the Earth?

What is gravity?

Gravity is a pulling force. It is a force that pulls any two masses towards each other. The bigger the mass, the more it pulls.

When you jump in the air, the Earth pulls you and you pull the Earth. The Earth is more massive so it does not appear to move. This is why you fall towards the Earth and not the other way round.

Sir Isaac Newton did a lot of work on gravity and helped us understand how it works. People say he had the idea when he saw an apple fall from a tree in his garden.

He used his ideas to explain why the Moon goes round the Earth and the Earth goes round the Sun.

How much do you weigh on Earth?

First you need to know your mass in kg.

Then you need to know that the Earth's gravity pulls each kilogram with a force of 10 N.

Then all you have to do is multiply those two numbers together.

So a person with a mass of 60 kg will have a weight of 600 N.

$60 \text{ kg} \times 10 = 600 \text{ N}$

d What is the weight of a person with a mass of 50 kg?

QUESTIONS

Copy these sentences and fill in the spaces using the words below:

> Earth   force   kilograms
> material   newtons

Mass is measured in _____. It tells us how much _____ an object has. Weight is measured in _____. It is the _____ of the _____ pulling an object towards its centre.

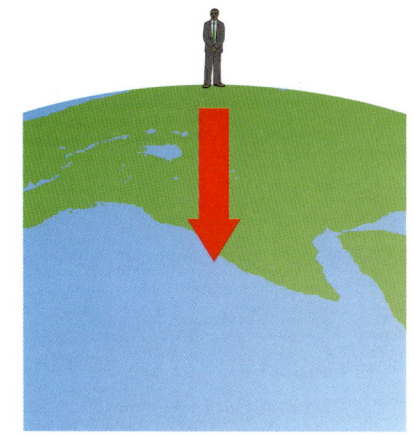

KEY POINTS

- Mass is measured in kilograms. It tells us how much material an object has.
- Weight is measured in newtons. It is the force of the Earth pulling the object towards it.

J2 HOW DOES GRAVITY CHANGE?

How much do you weigh on the Moon?

People weigh less on the Moon than on the Earth. Their mass is the same, they just weigh less. This is because the force of gravity on the Moon is less than on the Earth. The Moon pulls us towards it less than the Earth does. So we weigh less there.

Gravity on the Moon is about six times less than on the Earth. So a person standing on the Moon weighs about one-sixth as much as on Earth. This is because the Moon has one-sixth the gravitational field on its surface compared to the Earth.

Where else is gravity different?

Look at the table. It shows you how much an average person would weigh on different planets in the solar system. The differences in weight are because gravity is different on each of the planets.

Jupiter has more mass than the Earth, so gravity is stronger there. Pluto has less mass than the Earth, so gravity is weaker there.

Planet	Weight in N
Earth	600
Mars	122
Jupiter	1392
Pluto	36

a On which planet would a person weigh the most?

How does distance affect gravity?

Gravity gets less when objects move away from each other. The further apart they are, the weaker the force of gravity becomes.

- A 1 kg mass on the Earth's surface weighs 10 N.
- In space 14 000 km above the Earth, its weight would be only 1 N.
- If we took it far enough away from the Earth, it would have no weight at all.

b What happens to the Earth's gravity when we move away from the Earth into space?

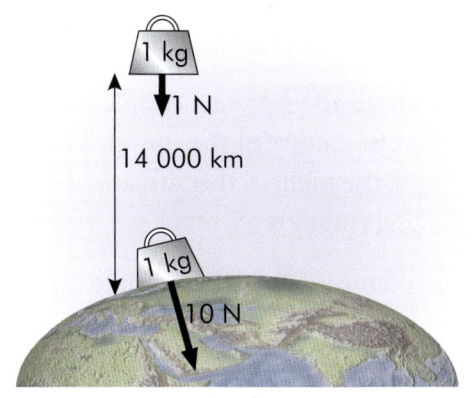

How do rockets leave the Earth?

When a rocket lifts off from the Earth to go into space, the rocket motors give an upwards **thrust**. This force must be greater than the force of gravity pulling the rocket back down.

As the rocket moves away from the Earth the force of gravity gets less. This makes it easier for the rocket motors to push against the force of gravity.

As the rocket uses up fuel, the mass of the rocket gets less. The rocket gets lighter. This also makes it easier for the rocket motors to push against the force of gravity.

c Why is it easier for a rocket motor to push against the Earth's gravity as the rocket heads into space?

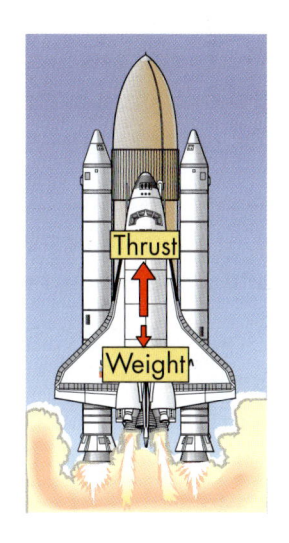

QUESTIONS

Copy these sentences and write **true** or **false** next to each one:

A mass of 1 kg will have the same mass if we put it on the Moon.

Gravity increases when two masses move apart.

The thrust of a rocket motor needs to be bigger than the force of the Earth's gravity for take-off.

KEY POINTS

- We would have different weights on different planets.
- The force of gravity gets smaller as objects get further apart.

J3 MODELS OF THE SOLAR SYSTEM

What did people believe in the past?

Hundreds of years ago, people believed that the Earth was at the centre of the universe. They thought that the Moon, the planets, the Sun and all the stars were moving round the Earth.

The picture shows what people thought the universe was like. You can see that they drew the Earth at the centre of the picture.

a Where did ancient people think the Earth was in the universe?

But there was a problem. They could not explain how the Sun and the planets moved in the sky. No matter how hard they tried, the movements of the Sun and planets just did not seem to fit the model.

A man called Copernicus lived about 1500. He thought that the Earth and all the planets went round the Sun. The picture shows this, with the Sun at the centre.

Another scientist called Galileo agreed with him. Galileo got into a lot of trouble because of his beliefs. The Roman Catholic Church condemned him for this. It was only a few years ago that the Church admitted that they were wrong.

b Which scientist first thought that the Earth went round the Sun?

What is the model that we use today?

About 400 years ago a scientist call Kepler thought about it some more. He worked out that the Earth and the planets **orbit** (go round) the Sun. The orbits are **elliptical** (not quite round).

c What do we call the paths taken by the Earth and planets going round the Sun?

Look at the picture. You can see the shape of the orbits as the planets go round the Sun.

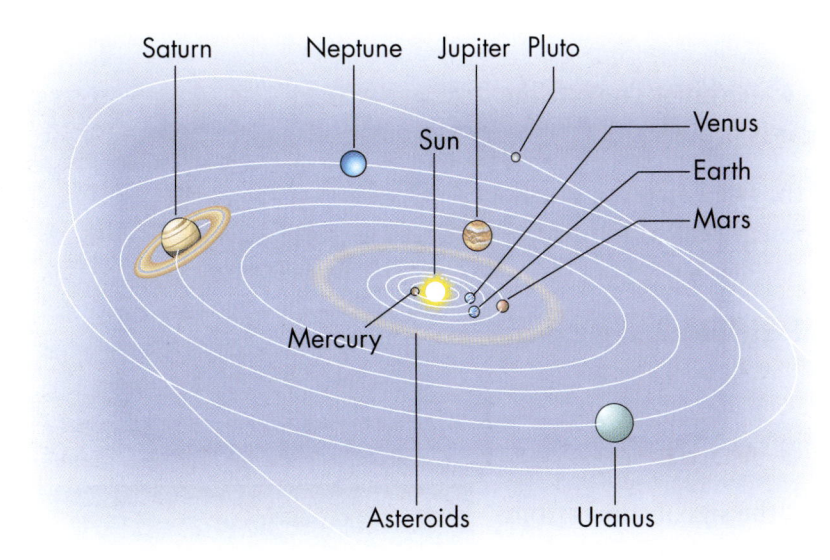

What orbits what?

The force of gravity from the Sun is 330 000 times more powerful than the force of gravity on the Earth. Just imagine how much you would weigh if you could walk on the surface of the Sun. The Sun's gravity is so great because it is very big with a huge mass.

The Sun's gravity pulls the Earth towards the Sun. This is what keeps the Earth orbiting the Sun.

d **What keeps the moon orbiting the Earth?**

Look at the boy in the picture. The string is like the force of gravity. It keeps the mass swinging round the boy, so it can't fly off.

QUESTIONS

Copy these sentences and fill in the spaces using the words below:

Copernicus   gravity   orbit

A scientist called _____ was the first person to think that the Earth went round the Sun. We now know that all the planets _____ the Sun. They stay in their orbits because of the force of _____.

KEY POINTS

- People used to think that the Earth was the centre of the universe.
- We now know that the Earth goes round the Sun.
- The force of gravity keeps the Earth and the planets orbiting the Sun, and the Moon orbiting the Earth.

Gravity and space

J4 SATELLITES

What are satellites?

A **satellite** is an object that orbits something. The satellite has a smaller mass than the thing it is orbiting.

The Moon is a satellite of the Earth. The Earth is a satellite of the Sun. The Earth and the Moon are called **natural satellites**.

Scientists can now make **artificial satellites** and put them into orbit around the Earth.

What kinds of orbits do we use?

When people watch Sky television, the signal comes from a satellite. The satellite stays in the same place in the sky, so we do not lose the signal.

The satellite takes one day to orbit the Earth. The Earth also turns round once in a day beneath it. So the satellite always stays above the same point on the Earth, and our satellite dish is always pointing in the right direction. The picture below shows a satellite that always stays above America, so people there can receive its signal.

Other satellites take much less than a day to orbit the Earth. They seem to move across the sky. The new space station is like this. On a clear night, if you are lucky, you can see the space station move across the sky like a bright star.

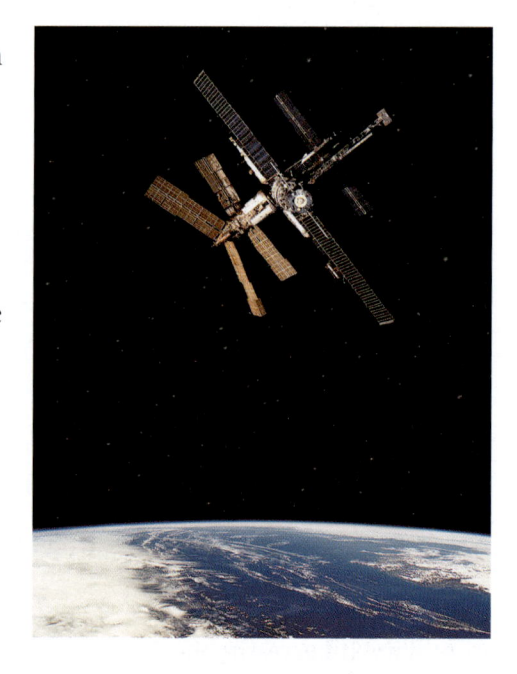

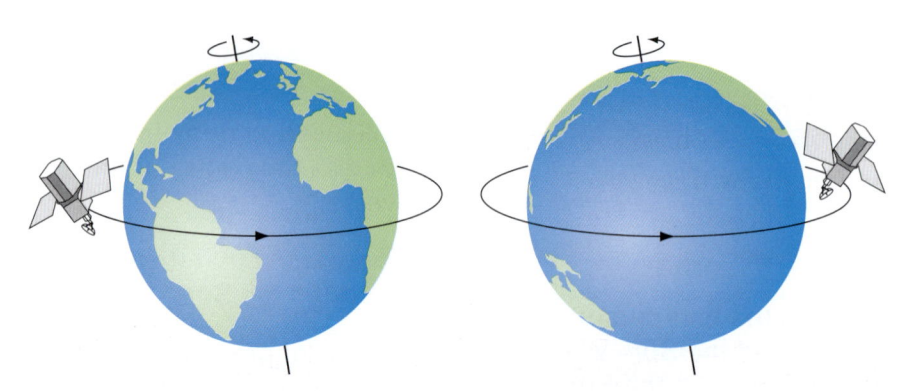

a What kind of satellite orbits the Earth once a day?

What is the history of satellites?

The first satellite was launched in 1957. Since then hundreds of different satellites have been sent up.

Some of them have fallen back to Earth. They usually burn up safely in the Earth's atmosphere before they hit the ground.

Look at the table. It shows some of the most important satellites that have been launched, and what job they do.

Name	Launch date	Job
Sputnik 1	4 October 1957	none
US Tiros 1	1 February 1958	first weather satellite
Early Bird	6 April 1965	geostationary satellite for TV and phone calls
GPS satellites	March 1994	tell people exactly where they are on the Earth's surface

How are satellites different?

Communications satellites are **geostationary satellites**. They stay in the same place above the Earth's surface. We use them for sending TV and phone signals all around the world.

- **Polar satellites** orbit the Earth from pole to pole. They are used for studying the weather. They are not much good for TV or phone signals as they keep disappearing from sight.

- **Low Earth orbit satellites** are sometimes called spy satellites. They can take very clear pictures of what is happening on the ground.

- **Global positioning satellites** (GPS) tell us exactly where we are on the ground. Some cars have a receiver so drivers can tell where they are to within just a few metres. This makes navigation much more accurate. And fun as well!

QUESTIONS

Make a list of all the different kinds of satellite and the jobs that they do.

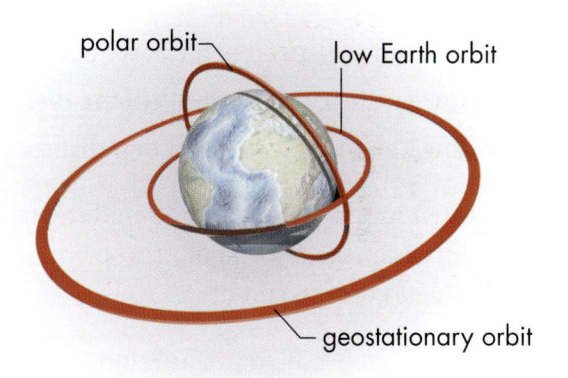

KEY POINTS

- Satellites can be placed in different orbits.
- Different satellites do different jobs.

K Speeding up

K1 HOW FAST IS IT MOVING?

Why do we measure speed?

Car drivers need to know how fast they are moving. It is important that they do not break the speed limit. The speedometer in the car tells the driver how fast they are going.

How is speed calculated?

To work out the **speed** of a car, we need to know two things:

1. how far the car has travelled: the **distance**
2. how long it took to travel that distance: the **time**.

We often measure how long something takes to travel a certain distance. In a 100 metres sprint, we time how long the athletes take to run it.

Look at the table. It shows how long eight different athletes took to run 100 metres.

a Which athlete won the race?

We can work out the speed of each athlete. To calculate speed we use this formula:

$$\text{speed} = \frac{\text{distance}}{\text{time}}$$

Scientists usually measure distance in **metres** and time in **seconds**.

b In what units do scientists usually measure distance and time?

Athlete	Time in seconds
1	10.45
2	11.51
3	10.00
4	10.40
5	11.00
6	10.26
7	11.04
8	11.11

Look at the table again. Athlete 5 ran the 100 metres in 11 seconds.

Look at the formula for speed. We divide the distance by the time to calculate the speed of the athlete.

$$\text{speed} = \frac{100}{11} = 9.09 \text{ metres per second}$$

Scientists usually shorten 'metres per second' to m/s.

c **Calculate the speed of athlete 3.**

How can we measure speed?

We can measure speed in all sorts of ways. The police often use a radar 'gun' to check the speed of motorists.

In school we measure speed using **light gates**. These time how quickly something moves between two points. The trolley in the picture is about to go through a light gate.

QUESTIONS

1 If a bird flies 200 metres in 100 seconds, what is its speed?

2 If a cheetah runs 60 metres in 3 seconds, what is its speed?

KEY POINTS

- We calculate speed by dividing distance by time.

Speeding up

K2 GETTING FASTER

Faster and faster

Sometimes the speed of an object changes. Sometimes it moves faster and faster.

Look at the picture of James on his bike. At the top of the hill he was moving slowly. As he went down the hill his speed increased. Near the bottom of the hill he is moving very quickly. Scientists call this change of speed **acceleration**.

a What do we call a change of speed?

Look at the picture of the trolley. It is rolling down a slope and accelerating. It has just passed through one light gate. It is about to pass through a second light gate. By using two light gates we can find out how the trolley is accelerating.

b Why are we using two light gates in the picture?

What happens when the slope is steeper?

James notices that when he is moving down a very steep slope he speeds up more.

The steeper the slope, the greater the acceleration.

c Which gives a bigger acceleration, a gentle slope or a steep slope?

Speeding up

What happens when the object is heavier?

One day James is freewheeling down the hill with his friend Sonata. Sonata is much lighter than James. James thinks because he is heavier, he will reach the bottom of the hill first. But they both reach the bottom at the same time.

James is confused. He decides to do an experiment. He goes up to his bedroom window and drops two objects at exactly the same time. One of them is a lead ball. The other is an aluminium ball. The lead ball is much heavier than the aluminium ball.

James thinks the lead ball will hit the ground first. Sonata waits outside and carefully watches the two balls fall to the ground.

d **Do you think James is right? Will the heavy lead ball hit the ground first?**

In fact, gravity makes the balls fall together so they hit the ground at the same time.

Measuring time precisely

Modern timers can measure time very precisely.

James could use light gates and an electronic timer to measure the time it takes the metal balls to hit the ground. He would still find that both balls would hit the ground at the same time.

QUESTIONS

Copy these sentences and write **true** or **false** next to each one:

When an object travels at the same speed we say it is accelerating.

If you drop two heavy balls out of a window they will land at the same time.

KEY POINTS

- When objects change speed we say they are accelerating.
- Gravity makes objects accelerate.

Speeding up

K3 HOW DO FORCES AFFECT SPEED?

How can things travel at a steady speed?

We are used to things slowing down when we move them. If we roll a ball along the ground, it slows and comes to a stop. If we stop pedalling on a bicycle, we slow down and stop.

This happens because other forces slow us down. Friction between the tyres and the road slows us down when we are moving. There is also friction with the air as we move through it. We have to push the air out of the way. This is called **air resistance**.

But in space, there is no friction or air resistance because there is no air. In space, once an object is moving, it carries on moving. It stays moving in the same direction and at the same speed until some other force acts upon it.

Look at the picture. It is an asteroid. It carries on moving through space at the same speed, because there is nothing to slow it down.

a Why does the asteroid in the picture not slow down?

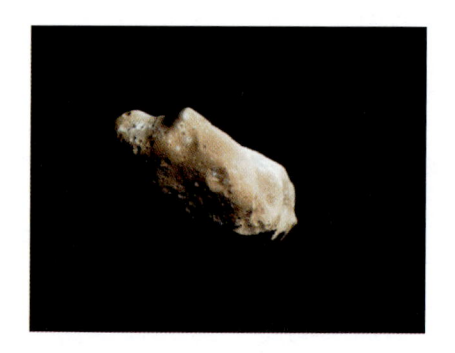

What happens when forces are balanced?

Look at Jane pushing the shopping trolley. Her push equals the forces of friction from the wheels. The trolley is moving at a constant speed because the forces are balanced.

If she stops pushing, the friction from the wheels will slow the trolley down until it stops.

b Why is the shopping trolley moving at a constant speed?

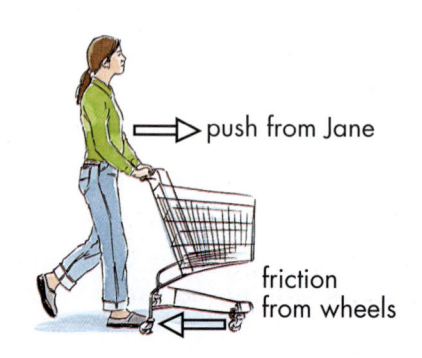

Speeding up

Look at this picture. The children are both pushing the trolley in opposite directions. Both their pushes are equally hard. The forces are balanced so the trolley does not move.

The two pictures of the shopping trolley tell us about **balanced forces**. If forces are balanced, the object carries on doing the same thing. If it is moving, it carries on at the same speed. If it is not moving, it stays not moving.

How do unbalanced forces affect movement?

The shopping trolley will only speed up, slow down, or change direction, when there are **unbalanced forces**.

Imagine Jane pushing the trolley along at a constant speed. Her pushing balances the friction of the wheels. The trolley moves at a constant speed in a straight line.

Mark comes along and pushes from the side. The forces are no longer balanced and the trolley changes direction.

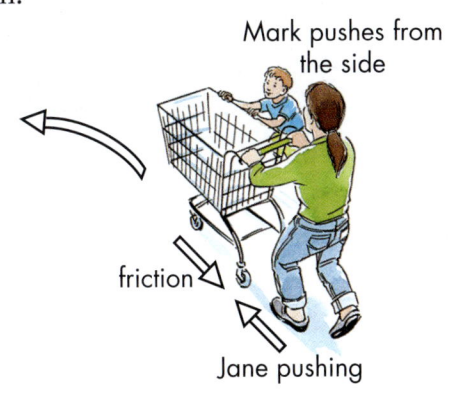

c If Mark had pushed the trolley from the front, would it have changed direction?

QUESTIONS

Copy these sentences and fill in the spaces using the words below:

> balanced   unbalanced

The speed or direction of an object does not change if the forces are _____.

If the forces are _____, the speed or direction of an object will change.

KEY POINTS

- If forces are balanced, the speed and direction does not change.
- Speed and direction only change when the forces are unbalanced.

Speeding up

K4 HOW CAN WE INCREASE SPEED?

How does shape help?

As you move through the air, there is friction with the air. This is air resistance and it slows you down.

To reduce air resistance, racing cyclists lower their bodies and wear helmets with a special shape. Look at the helmet. It is rounded at the front and pointed at the back. This is called a **streamlined** shape.

a What do we call a shape that has very little air resistance?

Resistance is also a problem in the water. Look at the submarine and the whale. They are also round at the front and pointed at the back. Just like the helmet on the racing cyclist, they have a streamlined shape.

b Why do the whale and the submarine have a streamlined shape?

How does speed affect air resistance?

Even the most streamlined objects still have some air resistance. The faster they move, the more air resistance there is. When a car moves, there is air resistance.

Look at the table. It shows how much petrol a car uses to travel 100 km at different speeds.

Speed	Petrol used
60 km/h	6 litres per 100 km
80 km/h	7.5 litres per 100 km

c Does the car use more petrol to travel 100 km at 60 km/h or at 80 km/h?

The faster a car travels, the more petrol it uses to cover the same distance. Or put another way…
Cars are more economical at a slower speed.

d **If you want to save petrol is it best to drive quickly or slowly?**

A car uses more petrol when it travels quickly because the air resistance is greater. So it needs more force to overcome the extra air resistance.

Why does a spacecraft get hot when it re-enters the atmosphere?

When a spacecraft re-enters the Earth's atmosphere it is moving very fast. There is a lot of air resistance as it pushes air out of the way. There is friction between the air particles and the spacecraft. This causes the surface of the spacecraft to become very hot.

Try rubbing your hands together. It will make them feel hot. The same thing happens when the air particles rub against the surface of the spacecraft.

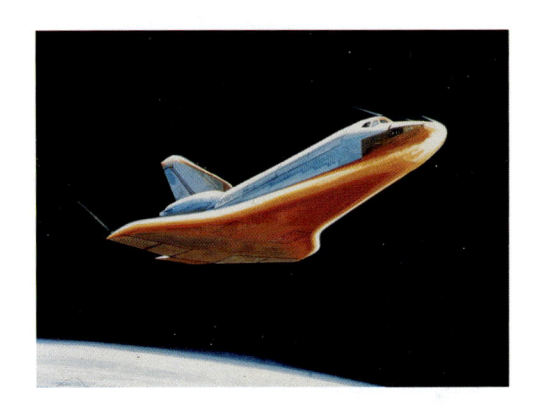

QUESTIONS

Copy and complete the crossword.

1 across Cars use more petrol when they go …
1 down This makes things hot when they rub against each other.
2 across A shape with little air resistance.
3 across Air _____ increases as things go faster.

KEY POINTS

- Streamlined shapes reduce air resistance.
- At high speed the friction caused by air resistance can make things hot.

Speeding up

K5 HOW DO PARACHUTES WORK?

What is freefall parachuting?

When this parachutist jumps from a plane, he falls faster and faster. He is accelerating. This is because the forces are unbalanced.

The force of gravity (his weight) pulls him down. This force is greater than the force of air resistance.

But as he gets faster the force of air resistance increases. Eventually the force of air resistance is the same as the force of his weight. The forces are now balanced. The parachutist falls at a constant speed.

a When does the parachutist fall at a constant speed?

What does a parachute do?

The parachutist is now travelling very quickly. If he were to hit the ground at this speed he would die. He must slow down before he hits the ground.

He opens his parachute. He slows down a lot. This is because the parachute is very large. It gives a very big air resistance.

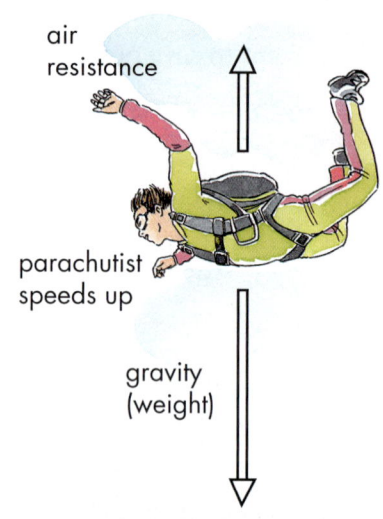

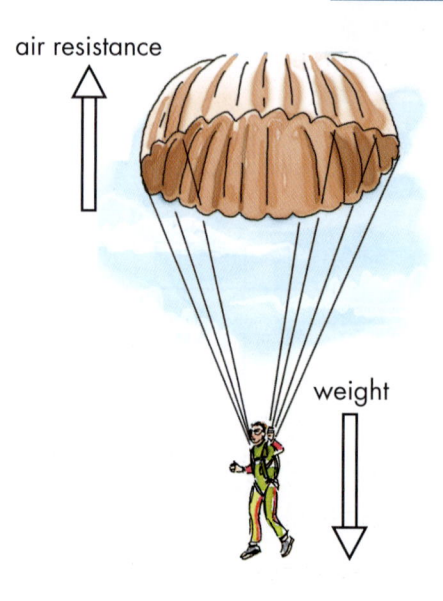

Speeding up

Parachutes are very good at slowing down things that are moving very quickly. Look at the picture of the space shuttle. When it lands it is travelling very fast. It uses parachutes to slow it down quickly.

QUESTIONS

Look at the two diagrams. One parachutist has a large parachute. One has a small parachute.

Which parachutist will fall faster?

Which parachutist will take longer to reach the ground?

KEY POINTS

- There are two forces on a freefalling parachutist, weight and air resistance.
- The parachutist will accelerate until the force of air resistance is the same as the force of his weight.
- Parachutes make the air resistance bigger. This means things fall slower.

Speeding up

L Pressure and moments

L1 WHAT IS PRESSURE?

Pressure, force and area

Forces can make objects move and change direction. Forces can have other effects too. When a force pushes on a solid object it causes **pressure**.

When you push a drawing pin into a board you create pressure.

Look at the picture. At the flat pin head the force is spread out over a large area. This means the pressure on the finger is small. At the point, the same force is concentrated on a tiny area. This means the pressure on the board is high.

We can write this more simply by saying:

- The same force on a large area gives low pressure.
- The same force on a small area gives high pressure.

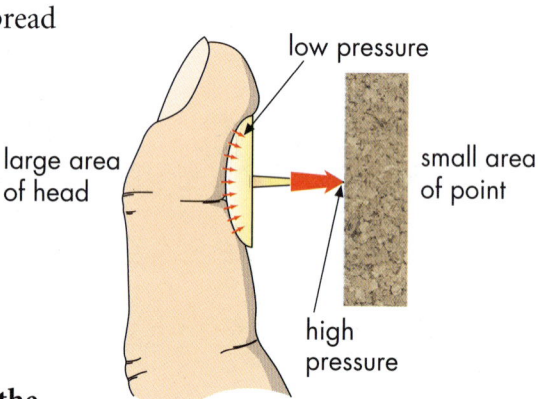

a If the force is concentrated onto a small area, is the pressure high or low?

How do we calculate pressure?

This is easier than you might think. We simply divide the force by the area.

$$\text{pressure} = \frac{\text{force}}{\text{area}}$$

The answer we get is in **pascals**. These are units named after a scientist called Blaise Pascal. We write them Pa for short.

b What unit do we use for measuring pressure?

What is the pressure under our feet?

Let's look at an example.
Jo weighs 500 N. Her feet have a surface area of 0.02 m².
Look at the formula for pressure again. If we divide 500 by 0.02 we get:

$$\text{pressure of Jo's feet on the floor} = \frac{500}{0.02} = 25\,000 \text{ Pa}$$

This may look a big number but it's really quite a small pressure. So Jo's feet do not sink into the floor.

Jo decides to wear her stiletto-heeled shoes. When she stands on her stilettos, the surface area of each heel is only 1 cm². (That's just 0.0001 m².)

If we calculate the pressure of her stiletto heels on the floor we find:

    pressure of Jo's stiletto heels on the floor = 5 000 000 Pa

This a much bigger number. If Jo walks on a wooden floor her stiletto heels will sink into it. The owner of the floor will not be very pleased.

Pressure is important for other animals.

Camels walk on soft sand in the desert. To stop them sinking into the sand they have very large feet. The big feet spread the force out over a larger surface. This means less pressure, so their feet do not sink into the sand.

People who live in cold places have to walk on soft snow. They have small feet and will sink into the snow. To reduce the pressure they wear snow-shoes. This makes a much larger surface pressing into the snow. The pressure is less so they do not sink into the snow.

Camels have big feet.

QUESTIONS

An elephant's foot exerts a pressure of 60 000 Pa on the floor. Would it be more dangerous to be stood on by an elephant or by Jo's stiletto heel?

KEY POINTS

- Pressure = $\dfrac{\text{force}}{\text{area}}$

L2 WHAT IS HYDRAULICS?

Hydraulics

Hydraulics is about how liquids behave when under pressure.

Look at the picture of the two syringes. They are connected together by a rubber tube. They are also filled with water. When the plunger in the first syringe is pushed inwards, the plunger in the second syringe moves outwards.

a What will happen to the plunger in the first syringe if we push in the plunger in the second syringe?

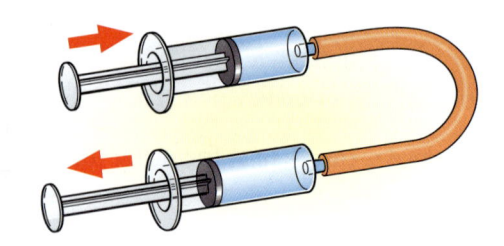

Hydraulic systems

Using car brakes is similar to the two syringes. Instead of syringes there are **pistons** which are almost the same. The first piston is connected to the brake pedal. The second piston is connected to the brakes. When we press the brake pedal, the brakes go on.

But there is a problem. If we use two pistons of the same size, we have to push very hard indeed to make the brakes work. This makes driving very difficult.

Fortunately there is an answer to the problem.

The piston attached to the brake pedal is very small. The piston attached to the brakes is very big. You push the brake pedal with a small force. You get a much bigger force on the brakes. We call this **force amplification**.

b What do we call it when a small force on a small piston produces a large force on a large piston?

Pressure and moments

Look at the picture. It shows how force amplification helps us put on the brakes in a car.

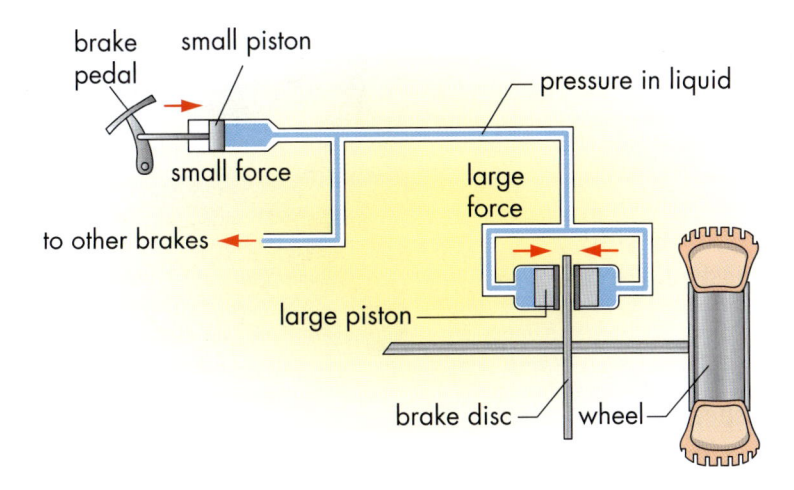

It sounds as though we are getting something for nothing. But we know that this is impossible.

This is what really happens.

The small piston has to move a long way with little force.

The large piston may have more force, but it only moves a small distance.

So the brake pedal moves a small force through a large distance.

And the brakes move a large force through a small distance.

C When a car driver presses the brake pedal, is the force on the brakes smaller or larger than the force of the driver's foot?

QUESTIONS

Copy these sentences choosing only the correct words:

When a car driver applies the brakes, she uses a **small / large** force. This applies a **large / small** force on the brakes. The brake pedal piston is **smaller / larger** than the piston attached to the brakes.

KEY POINTS

- Hydraulics are used to transfer forces from a brake pedal to the brakes.
- Hydraulics can be used to increase forces.

Pressure and moments

L3 WHAT IS PNEUMATICS?

Pneumatics

Pneumatics is about how gases behave when under pressure. You probably have a pneumatic tyre on your bicycle. Pneumatic tyres are pumped up with air. The air in the tyre is under pressure.

When air is put under pressure it behaves differently from water. Unlike water, air can be squashed. We call this **compressing** the air.

Look at the picture of the sealed syringe. When you push the plunger in, the air is squashed. The particles of air get pushed closer together.

a What happens to the particles of air in the sealed syringe when the plunger is pushed in?

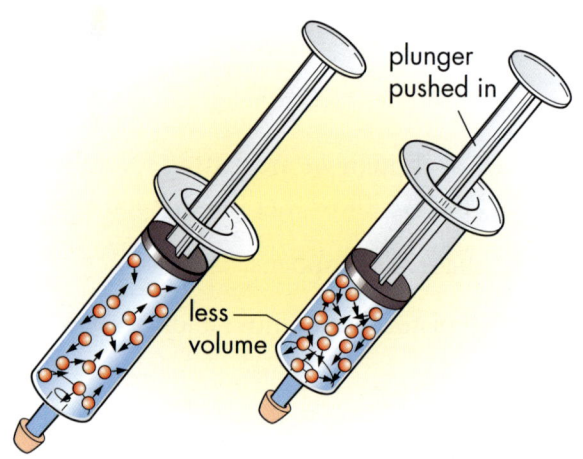

What causes gas pressure in a container?

To understand why gas has pressure, we need to think of the gas as lots of particles. Look at the picture of the particles of gas in a container. The particles of gas are crashing into the inner surface of the container. This is what causes the gas pressure.

Imagine we made the container smaller but kept the number of air particles the same. The same number of particles would be crashing into a smaller surface area. The pressure would increase.

b What will happen to the pressure in the sealed syringe when we push the plunger in?

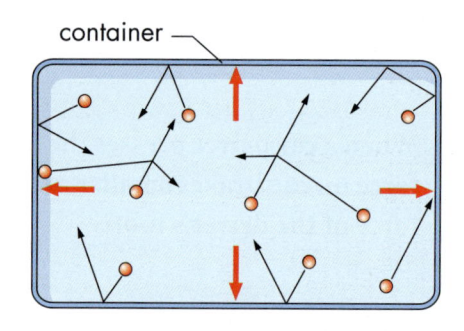

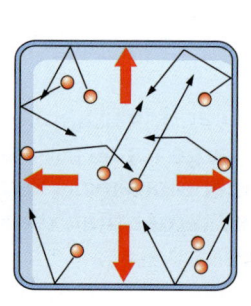

How do aerosols work?

An aerosol is half filled with a liquid and half filled with a gas under pressure. When we press the button, a valve opens and the gas under pressure forces out the liquid.

C How does the liquid come out of an aerosol?

What else can gas pressure be used for?

When you heat water, it turns into steam. Steam has gas pressure. The pressure of the steam can be used for driving steam engines. It also drives the turbines in a power station.

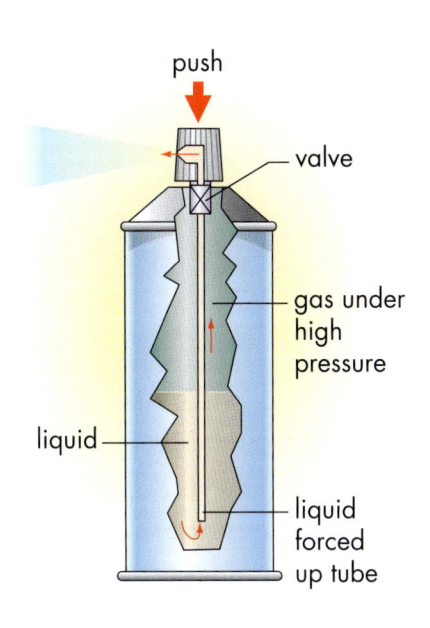

Atmospheric pressure

Gas does not have to be inside a container to have pressure.

We live on the surface of the Earth. We are at the bottom of an 'ocean' of air. There is a lot of air pressing on us. We call this **atmospheric pressure**.

When we climb to the top of a mountain there is less air pressing on us. So the air pressure at the top of the mountain is less than at the bottom of the mountain.

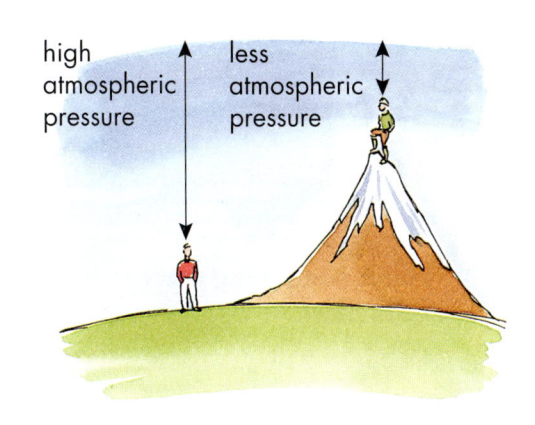

QUESTIONS

Copy these sentences and fill in the spaces using the words below:

> increase   particles   pressure

Gas pressure is caused by the _____ of the gas moving. If we squash the gas into a smaller space the pressure will _____. If we increase the amount of gas in a container, the _____ will also increase.

KEY POINTS

- Gases have pressure.

Pressure and moments

L4 HOW DO LEVERS WORK?

Levers

A **lever** is a very simple machine. It helps us to do things.

To understand how a lever works we need to know three things:

1. The lever turns around a point called the **pivot**. The lever usually goes down on one side of the pivot and up on the other side.
2. We push one side of the lever down. Our force is called the **effort**.
3. The lever moves up on the other side. It moves an object. Its force to do this is called the **load**. The load is the weight of the object that is moved.

a What is the point called around which a lever turns?

Look at the diagram of the lever.

It shows you where the pivot, effort and load are.

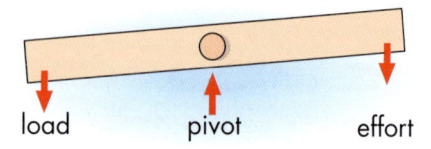

Look at the diagram. It shows a screwdriver being used to open a tin of paint. The screwdriver is being used as a lever.

b Name something that can be used as a lever.

How do levers amplify forces?

Try this…

On a door, the pivot is the hinge. The boy in the blue shirt is a long way from the pivot. He does not have to push very hard.

The boy in the green shirt is close to the pivot. He has to push as hard as he can.

It is the same with the screwdriver opening the tin of paint. The handle is a long way from the pivot. It is easy to push. The blade of the screwdriver is close to the pivot. It exerts a very big force on the tin lid.

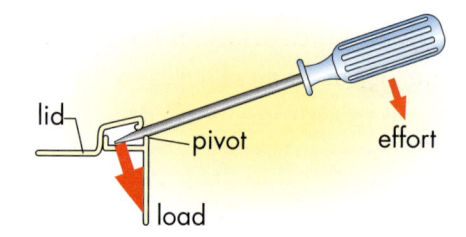

Levers are everywhere

Levers are all around us.

Using a spanner is an example of a lever.

Even chewing our food uses a lever. That's why we can easily crush things with our teeth.

Even our arms are levers.

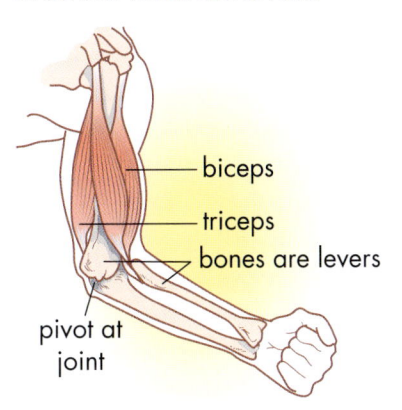

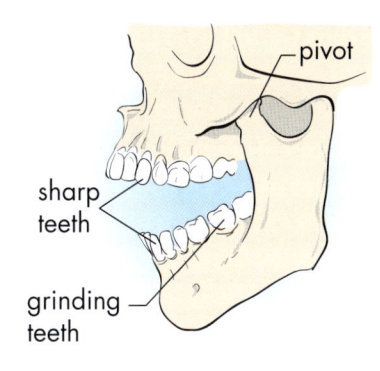

How much force can the screwdriver produce as a lever?

The answer is … a lot. In the most powerful levers, the effort is a long way from the pivot, and the load is close to the pivot.

Imagine that the screwdriver could not get the lid off the paint tin. If we used a longer screwdriver, the lid would come off much more easily.

A famous scientist once said that if he had a lever long enough he could move the world. It would have to be a very long lever.

QUESTIONS

Copy these sentences and fill in the spaces using the words below:

effort   load   pivot

Levers turn about a point called the _____.
The force we apply to the lever is called the _____. The lever moves a weight called the _____.

KEY POINTS

- We use levers to make forces bigger.

Pressure and moments

L5 USING COUNTERWEIGHTS

How do things balance?

Seesaws can help us to understand how things balance.

Look at the seesaws. The first one balances because both children are the same weight and the same distance from the pivot.

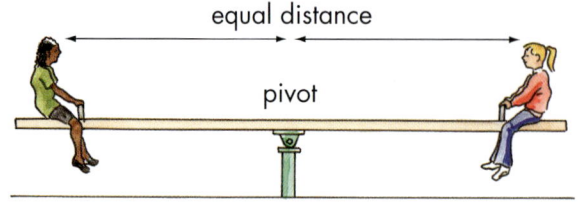

The seesaw below does not balance because the man is heavier than the boy.

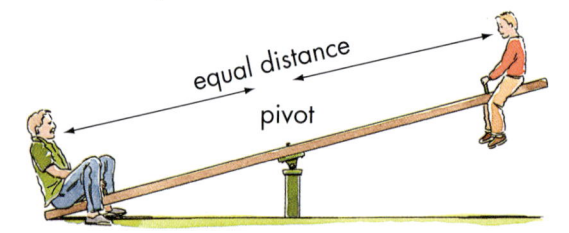

The seesaw below balances because the man has moved closer to the pivot.

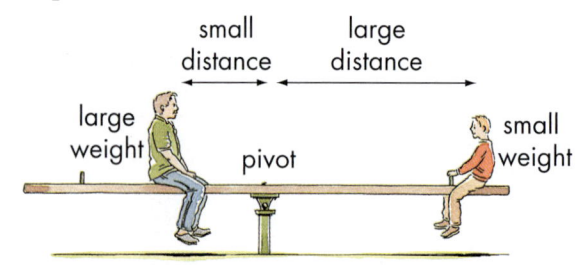

a What would happen to the seesaw if the man got off?

Balancing in life

Look at the picture of the kangaroo jumping. Its body is leaning forward. It does not fall over because the body is being balanced by the long tail.

Look at the picture of the pterodactyl. It has a very heavy beak. Its head does not fall forward because it has a long spur on the back of its head to balance its beak.

The kangaroo's tail and the spur on the head of the pterodactyl are called **counterbalances**.

b Look at the man ice-skating. What is he using for a counterbalance to stop him falling forwards?

Cranes also use a counterbalance. They can lift very heavy loads without falling over. In the picture below, the counterbalance stops the crane falling over when it lifts the weight.

c Why does the crane need a counterbalance?

How to lift safely

When some people lift a weight they lean forwards. If you lift with a bent back it produces very large forces on the spine and can damage it.

Sensible people lift with a straight back and bent legs.

d Which girl is lifting the box correctly, the girl on the left or the girl on the right?

QUESTIONS

Copy the seesaw below. Draw a person on the seat. They must be the right size to make the seesaw balance.

KEY POINTS

- For a seesaw to balance, a heavier person has to be closer to the pivot.
- Counterbalances are often used to make things balance.

L6 MOMENTS

What is a moment?

Seesaws are like levers. The force of your weight on the seesaw makes the seesaw turn about the pivot. This turning effect is called a **moment**.

When will a seesaw balance?

This is quite an easy question to answer.

Look at the diagram. We multiply the force by the distance from the pivot. We do this on both sides of the seesaw. The results should always be equal when the seesaw balances.

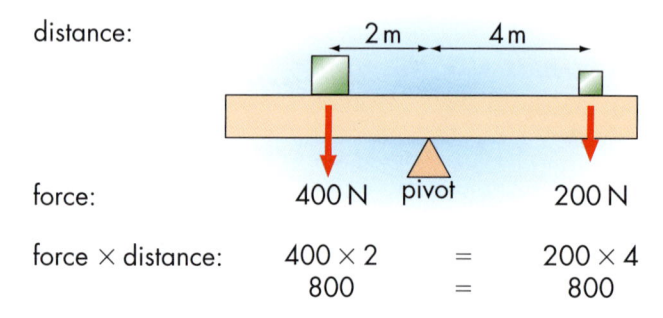

distance:	2 m		4 m
force:	400 N (pivot)		200 N
force × distance:	400 × 2	=	200 × 4
	800	=	800

This means the turning moment on the left-hand side of the seesaw is the same as the turning moment on the right-hand side of the seesaw.

Here is the diagram of the boy and man on a seesaw again.

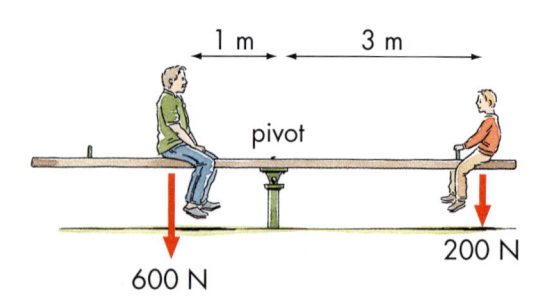

(Diagram: man 600 N at 1 m from pivot, boy 200 N at 3 m from pivot)

(Diagram: 400 N at 2 m, 200 N at 4 m, moment 800 Nm each side)

a Multiply the force by the distance for the man. Do the same for the boy. Do they balance?

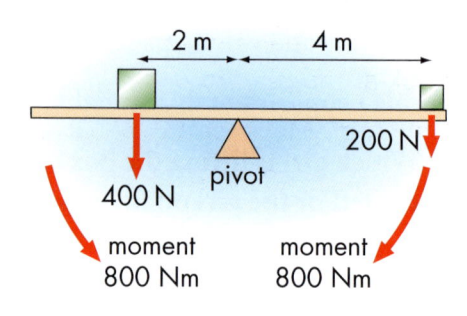

Moments and levers

L6

On page 118 you saw a screwdriver used to get the lid off a tin of paint.

We can calculate the force of the screwdriver blade on the tin lid. The moments on both sides are the same.

We push down on the handle with a force of 10 N. The distance from the handle to the pivot is 20 cm.

But the distance from the pivot to the blade is only 1 cm. The force on the lid is 200 N. It is no wonder that the lid comes off.

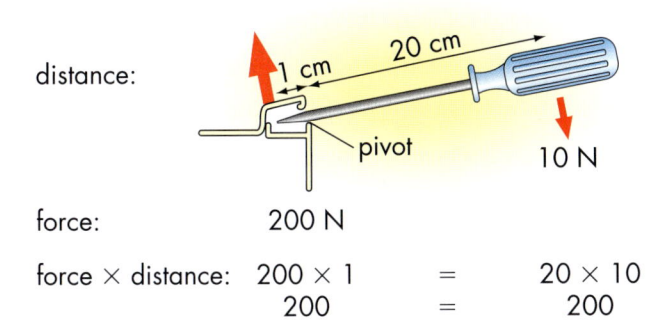

distance: 1 cm, 20 cm, 10 N, pivot

force: 200 N

force × distance: 200 × 1 = 20 × 10
                   200   = 200

QUESTIONS

Look at the picture.

Which of the seesaws will balance?

A: 200 N — 200 N

B: 200 N — 100 N

C: 200 N (1 m) — 100 N (2 m)

KEY POINTS

- The turning effect of a force on a lever is called a moment.
- For a seesaw to balance the moments on both sides of the seesaw must be the same.

Pressure and moments

Glossary

acceleration — a change in **speed**

acid rain — rainwater with gases dissolved in it that make it more acidic

addictive — when a **drug** makes someone feel ill if they don't take the drug

air resistance — friction with the air as something moves through it

alkali — a **base** that is soluble in water

antagonistic pair — a pair of muscles that pull a bone in opposite directions

application rate — how much fertiliser a farmer should use

artificial satellites — **satellites** put into **orbit** by people

asexual reproduction — reproduction that does not involve sex or sex cells

atmospheric pressure — force on an area caused by air particles bouncing off a surface

balanced — an equation is balanced when there are the same number of each kind of atom on each side

balanced diet — a diet that contains the correct balance of nutrients to stay healthy

balanced forces — when all forces are equal and the object carries on doing the same thing

ball and socket joint — a joint that moves in all directions, like the hip joint

base — the opposite of an acid: a base **neutralises** an acid

biomass — the **mass** of a living thing. It is usually measured dry (removing the water).

breathing system — the organ system where oxygen from the air enters the blood, and carbon dioxide is removed from the blood

carnivores — animals that eat only other animals

catalytic converter — a device fitted to a car exhaust that removes **pollutants**

chemical energy — energy stored in chemicals

chemical weathering — rocks being **weathered** by reacting with acidic rainwater

chlorophyll — the green substance in plants that allows them to make food

circulatory system — the organ system that pumps blood around the body

clones — identical copies of living things produced by **asexual reproduction**

competing	when living things live in the same place and need the same resources	**effort**	force applied to do a task, such as pushing a **lever**
compressing	squashing	**electrolyte**	a liquid that conducts electricity
conservation of energy	an idea that says that we cannot make or destroy energy, we can just change it from one form to another	**elliptical**	oval-shaped
		end point	the end of a **neutralisation** reaction, when the pH is 7
consumers	animals, which get their food by eating plants or other animals	**environmental variation**	features of a living thing that have been affected by its surroundings and lifestyle
contracting	getting shorter		
counterbalance	a **mass** used to balance the **weight** of another object	**fertilisers**	chemicals that provide the nutrients that plants need
deficiency	what happens to an animal or plant when it does not get enough of a certain nutrient	**fitness**	how well your heart and lungs supply oxygen to your body cells
		food chain	a diagram showing what eats what, and the flow of energy
digestive system	the organ system where food is taken in, broken down and absorbed into the blood	**food web**	a diagram with lots of **food chains** in a habitat joined together
displacement	a type of reaction where a metal is pushed out of its compound	**force amplification**	making a force bigger
distance	how far something has travelled	**fuel**	a substance that burns to release energy
drug	a chemical that affects the way your body works	**fuel cell**	a device that changes chemical energy into electrical energy
efficient	working without much waste		

Glossary

generator	a device that converts movement energy into electrical energy
genes	instructions that control a living thing's characteristics
geostationary satellite	**satellite** that stays in the same place above the Earth's surface
global positioning satellite (GPS)	**satellite** that allows people to find exactly where they are on the Earth's surface
global warming	the Earth getting warmer because of an increased **greenhouse effect**
gravity	a pulling force between two objects
greenhouse effect	a natural process that keeps the Earth warm
herbivores	animals that eat only plants
hinge joint	a joint that moves backward and forward, like the elbow joint
hydraulics	using liquids under **pressure**
hydrocarbon	a substance that contains only carbon and hydrogen
hydroxide	a substance formed when a metal reacts with water
inherit	when features are passed on from parent to offspring
inherited variation	features of a living thing that were passed on from its parents
insecticides	chemicals that kill insects
kilograms	units used to measure **mass**
lever	a simple machine that turns around a **pivot**
light gate	device that measures speed
load	force that is overcome to do a task, such as a **weight** that is lifted with a **lever**
low Earth orbit satellite	**satellite** that dips close to the Earth, and can take clear pictures of the Earth's surface
mains electricity	electricity supplied through power lines to our homes
mass	the amount of matter
metre	unit used to measure **distance**
model	an idea that helps us understand something that we cannot see
moment	the turning effect of a force: force multiplied by **distance** to the **pivot**
monitor	taking measurements to keep track of something
natural satellites	**satellites** such as the Moon and Earth
neutralisation	the reaction when an acid reacts with a **base**
newtons	units used to measure **weight**

omnivores	animals that eat both plants and animals	**pressure**	a force spread out over an area: pressure is force divided by area
orbit	a **mass** moving round another mass held by **gravity**	**producers**	plants, which make their own food by **photosynthesis**
ore	rocks found in the ground that contain metals	**reactivity series**	a list of substances in order of reactivity, with the most reactive first
organic farmers	farmers that do not use chemical **pesticides** or **fertilisers**	**respiration**	the chemical reaction that releases energy from glucose. The reaction also uses oxygen, and produces carbon dioxide and water.
organic material	any substance that comes from living things		
pascal	unit used to measure **pressure**		
pesticides	chemicals that kill **pests**	**salt**	a substance formed when an acid is **neutralised**
pests	animals that eat crops grown by farmers	**satellite**	an object that **orbits** another mass
photosynthesis	plants making food (glucose) from water and carbon dioxide using light energy. Oxygen and water are also produced.	**second**	unit used to measure **time**
		selective breeding	choosing features that we want in living things and breeding so that the offspring will have those features
physical weathering	rocks being **weathered** by changes in temperature		
piston	device like a syringe, used in **hydraulics**	**selective weedkiller**	a **weedkiller** that kills some kinds of plant but not others
pivot	point around which something turns	**sexual reproduction**	reproduction involving the male and female sex cells
pneumatics	using gases under **pressure**	**speed**	how fast something is travelling: the **distance** travelled divided by the **time** taken
polar satellite	**satellite** that **orbits** round the Earth's poles		
pollutants	substances that harm the environment	**sprain**	an injury caused by stretching a ligament

strain	an injury caused by hurting a muscle	**transferred**	energy is transferred when it is moved from one place to another
streamlined	a shape that does not give much **air resistance**	**transformed**	energy is transformed when it is changed from one form to another
tar	a mixture of chemicals in cigarette smoke that causes cancer	**turbine**	part of a power station where big fans turn as steam passes over them
tarnished	a metal that has reacted with air and is no longer shiny	**unbalanced forces**	when forces are not equal and the object's **speed** or direction changes
theory of conservation of mass	an idea that says that atoms cannot be created or destroyed in a chemical reaction	**voltage**	a measure of electrical push
		weathering	breaking down rocks by natural processes
thrust	a force that pushes something along	**weed**	a plant growing in the wrong place
time	how long something has taken	**weedkiller**	a chemical that kills **weeds**
trace elements	nutrients that are needed in small amounts by plants	**weight**	the force on something due to the Earth pulling on it

Index

Note: **bold** page numbers indicate **glossary** definitions

acceleration 104–5, 108–9, 110, **124**
acid rain 64, 66–9, **124**
acids
    and alkalis 48–9
    and carbonates 44–5
    carbonic 66
    hydrochloric 44, 45, 49, 56
    and metals 42–5, 50–1, 56–7, 65
    nitric 45, 66
    and oxides 46–7
    salts from reactions with 42–7, 49, 56, 65
    sulphuric 43, 45, 46, 50–1
addictive drugs 16–17, **124**
aerosols 117
air
    carbon dioxide in 20, 34, 66, 71
    pressure in tyre 116
    reactivity of metals with 52–3
    resistance 106, 108–9, 110, **124**
    see also gas; oxygen
alkalis 44, 54, **124**
    and acids 48–9
    and safety 48
    see also bases
aluminium 4
    ore 60
    reactivity 59, 60
alveoli 14
amphetamines 16
amplification 114–15, 118, **125**
animals
    camels' feet 113
    counterbalance 120
    dead, remains of 62
    manure from 32
    materials from 76
    selective breeding 6–7, **127**
    whale, shape of 108
    see also birds
antagonistic pair 19, **124**
application rate 32, **124**
area and pressure 112–13
arm 18, 19, 119
arthritis 19
artificial satellites 100, **124**
    geostationary 100, 101, **126**
    global positioning (GPS) 101, **126**
    Low Earth orbit 101, **126**
    polar 101, **127**
asexual reproduction 10, **124**
asteroids 99, 106
atmospheric pressure 117, **124**
atoms in chemical reactions 50–1, 78

balance/balanced
    counterbalance 120–1, **125**
    diet 13, **124**
    equations 50–1, **124**
    forces 106–7, **124**
    lack of (unbalanced) 107, **128**
ball and socket joint 18, **124**
bar charts 65
bases 44, 46, **124**
    dissolved in water see alkalis
    see also hydroxides
battery 74, 83, 84
bean 25
biceps 18, 119
bicycle 90, 106, 116
biomass 25, **124**
birds
    DDT in 37
    in food web 35, 36
    in pyramid of numbers 37
bones 18, 119
breathing system 12, 14, **124**
    and smoking 15
breeding, selective 6–9, **127**
bridges 41
burning see fuels

cactus 23
calcium 55, 56, 57
calcium carbonate 44, 45
calcium chloride 44, 45
camel 113
cancer, lung 15
cannabis 16
car see cars
carbohydrates in diet 13
carbon
    in electric cell 84
    reactivity 60
    see also hydrocarbons
carbon dioxide
    in air 20, 34, 66, 71
    from animals breathing 28
    from burning fuel 28
    and global warming 71
    from metal and acid reaction 44–5, 65
    and plants
        absorbed by trees 29
        for photosynthesis 20–1, 28, 38–9, 66
    in rainwater 66
    and respiration 12
carbon monoxide 73
carbonates and acids 44–5
carbonic acid 66
carnivores 30, **124**
cars
    brakes 114–15
    catalytic converter 69, **124**
    engine 74, 82
    fuel 108–9
    pistons 114–15, **127**
    speed 102, 103, 108–9
cartilage 18
catalytic converter 69, **124**
cattle breeding 7
cell
    electrical 74, 83, 84, 86
    fuel 75, 83, **125**
    human (egg and sperm) 2–3, 4
    plant 8–9, 26
cellulose 25
chalky soil 62
chemical, energy 82, 84, **124**
chemical reactions
    atoms in 50–1, 78
    in body 13
    see also reactivity of metals
chemical weathering 64–5, **124**
chewing 119
chloride 44, 45, 49, 56
chlorophyll 22–3, **124**
    magnesium for 27, 33
chloroplast 22
circuit, electrical 84, 85, 86, 87
circulatory system 12, **124**
clay soil 62
clones 10–11, **124**
coal 69, 73, 91
coins 41
cold, resistance to 8
competition/competing 34–5, **125**
compression/compressing 116, **125**
conduction
    electrical 40, 41

thermal 40, 89
conservation
   of energy 93, **125**
   of mass 79–81, **128**
   of rare breeds 7
consumers 30, **125**
   see also animals
contracting 19, **125**
convection 89
Copernicus 98
copper
   conductor of electricity 41
   for plants 33
   reactivity 57, 59, 60, 61, 78
   uses 61
copper oxide 46
copper sulphate 46, 47, 78
counterbalance 120–1, **125**
crane 121
crops see plants for food
crystal 47
current, electrical 84, 85, 86, 87
cuttings from plants 11

danger
   from alkalis 48
   from electricity 85
   from gas heaters 73
DDT 37
deficiency, food 13, **125**
diaphragm 14
diet, balanced 13, **124**
   see also food
digestive system 12, 13, **125**
diseases 19
displacement reactions 58–9, 74, **125**
dissolving
   bases in water see alkalis
   mass conserved when 79
distance **125**
   and gravity 97
   and moment 122, 123
   and speed 102–3
dogs, breeding 6
drugs 16–17, **125**
   addictive 16–17, **124**
   alcohol 17
dynamite 74

Earth and planets see solar system
ecstasy 16
efficiency/efficient 92–3, **125**
effort 118, **125**
egg cells
   in humans 2–3, 4
   in plants 8–9
elbow 18
electricity, hydroelectric 91

electricity/electrical energy 82–93
   amount used 88–9
   battery 74, 83, 84
   circuit 84, 85, 86, 87
   conduction 40, 41
   current 84, 85, 86, 87
   for metal extraction 60
   generation of 80–1, 90–1, **126**
   mains 88–9, **126**
   models 86–7
   power stations 69, 75, 90–1, 92, 117
   transferring energy 84–5
   useful 82–3
   voltage 85, 86, 87, 88, **128**
   wasted 89, 92–3
electrolyte 75, **125**
elements, trace **128**
elliptical orbit 98–9, **125**
embryo 4
end point 48–9, **125**
energy
   and breathing 14
   chemical 82, 84, **124**
   conservation of 93, **125**
   efficiency 92–3, **125**
   from food 12–13
   loss through friction 92, 106–7
   movement 74, 82
   and photosynthesis 20–1, 24
   sound 88
   transfer/transferred 82, 84–5, 89, **128**
   transformed 82, 84, 93, **128**
   wave 91
   wind 82, 91
   see also electricity; heat; light
environment/environmental chemistry 62–71
   see also acid rain; pollutants; rocks; soils
   and plants 28–9
   variation 5–6, **125**
epidermis of leaf 22
equations, balanced 50–1, **124**
exercise and sport 12, 14, 18–19, 121
explosions 74

falling 94
farming
   crops see plants for food
   organic 39, **127**
   selective breeding 7
   see also fertilisers
fat
   in diet 13
   in plants 25, 30, 76

fertilisation 4, 8–9
fertilisers 32–3, **125**
   application rate 32, **124**
fibre, cotton 25
fibre in diet 13
fitness and health 12–19, **125**
   breathing and smoking 14–15, **124**
   drugs and alcohol 16–17, **125**
   see also exercise
flowers 8–9, 27, 33
food
   balanced diet 13, **124**
   chain 30, **125**
   chewing 119
   deficiency 13, **125**
   energy from 12–13
   for plants see nutrients
   from plants see plants for food
   webs 30, 31–2, 35, 36, **125**
forces
   amplification 114–15, 118, **125**
   balanced 106–7, **124**
   and moment 122, 123
   and pressure 112–13
   pulling see gravity
   pushing 106–7
   and speed 106–7
   unbalanced 107, **128**
   see also pressure; weight
freefall parachuting 110
friction and energy loss 92, 106–7
fruit 8, 31, 63
fuel cell 75, 83, **125**
fuels, burning 28, **125**
   carbon dioxide from 28
   coal 69, 91
   gas 73, 82
   global warming and 71
   oil 76, 91
   and oxygen 72, 73
   wood 74

Galileo 98
gas
   cooking 82
   heaters, danger from 73
   under pressure (pneumatics) 116–17, **127**
   see also air; carbon dioxide; hydrogen; oxygen
generator 90, **126**
genes 3, 4, 7, **126**
geostationary satellites 100, 101, **126**
gerbil model of electricity 86
global positioning satellite (GPS) 101, **126**

global warming 71, **126**
glucose
    in diet 13
    from photosynthesis in plants
        20–1, 24–5, 30, 76
    in respiration 12, 24
    stored in plant *see* cellulose;
        starch
gold 40, 42
    nugget 60
    reactivity 52, 55, 57, 60, 61
    uses 61
GPS (global positioning satellite)
    101, **126**
graphite 40
gravity 94–5, **126**
    change 96–7
    and distance 97
    and speed 105, 110
    of Sun 99
greenhouse 21, 38–9
    effect 71, **126**
growth
    and food 12–13
    of plants 20–1, 27, 34–5
gunpowder 49

health *see* fitness
heart 12, 14
heat energy 74, 82, 88
    loss 89, 92, 93
    see also temperature
herbivores 30, **126**
heroin 16
hinge joint 18, **126**
hip joint 18
    artificial 19
hydraulics 114–16, **126**
hydrocarbons 72–3, **126**
    see also coal; oil
hydrochloric acid 44, 45, 49, 56
hydroelectricity 91
hydrogen
    produced from metal reactions
        42, 43, 50–1, 54, 56
    see also hydrocarbons
hydroxides 48, 49, 54, **126**

identical twins 4–5
illegal drugs 16
indicator 54
inheritance/inherit 2–11, **126**
    clones 10–11, **124**
    inherited variation 2–3, **126**
    selective breeding 6–9, **127**
insecticides 36, **126**
insulation 89
iodine test for starch 23, 24, 31

iron 41
    for plants 33
    reactivity 52, 56, 57, 58–9, 60, 78
iron oxide 59
iron sulphate 58, 74, 78

joints
    ball and socket 18, **124**
    hinge 18, **126**

kangaroo 120
Kepler, Johannes 98
kilograms 94, 95, **126**
kneecap 18

lakes and acid rain 69
lead 40, 45
lead sulphate 45
leaves
    and photosynthesis 22–5, 27
    veins 22, 27
leg 18
levers 118–19, 123, **126**
lichens 70
lifting safely 121
ligament 18
light energy 74, 88
    for photosynthesis in plants
        20–1, 24, 34, 38–9
light gates for measuring speed 103,
    104, **126**
lightning 85
lime 63
limestone 44
    weathering 64–5, 68
    see also calcium carbonate
limewater 44
lithium hydroxide 54
lithium, reactivity of 52–3, 54, 55,
    57
load **126**
Low Earth orbit satellite 101, **126**
lungs 12, 14, 15

magnesium
    in fertilisers 32
    for plants 27, 33
    reactivity 55, 56, 57, 59, 74, 80
magnesium carbonate 44
magnesium chloride 56
magnesium oxide 80
mains electricity 88–9, **126**
manure 32
marble (glass) model of electricity
    85, 86
marble (rock) 68
mass **126**
    conservation of 78–81, **128**

and gravity 94, 95, 96
measured in kilograms 94, 95,
    126
measurement
    of mass 94, 95, **126**
    of speed 102–3, 104, **126**
    of time 105
    of weight 94, 95, **126**
medical drugs 16
mercury 40, 81
mercury oxide 81
metals 40–51
    and acids 42–5, 50–1, 56–7, 65
    compounds *see* alkalis; balanced
        equations; carbonates;
        oxides
    ore **127**
    properties 40
    useful 40–1
    see also reactivity of metals
methane 72
metres 102, **126**
mice in food web 35, 36
minerals in diet 13
model **126**
    electricity 86–7
    solar system 98–9
moments 122–3, **126**
monitor 70, **126**
Moon 96, 100
movement energy 18–19, 74, 82
muscles 14, 19, 119
    antagonistic pair 19, **124**

natural satellites 96, 100, **126**
neutralisation 48–9, **126**
    end point 48–9, **125**
new materials 76–7
Newton, Sir Isaac 95
newtons 94, 95, **126**
nitrates 32, 45
nitric acid 45, 66
nitrogen 27, 33
nitrogen oxide 66–7
non-metals 41
nucleus of cell 3
nutrients for plants 27, 34, 38–9
    fertilisers 32–3, **125**
    transport 26

oil 76, 91
omnivores 30, **127**
orbit 98–9, **126**, **127**
    elliptical 98–9, **125**
    of satellites 101, **125**
ores 60, **127**
organic farmers 39, **127**
organic material 62, **127**

Index

ovary in plant 8
oxides 46–7, 59
oxygen 21
   and burning fuels 72, 73
   and conservation of mass 80
   for breathing in animals 28
   in greenhouse 21
   metal and acid reaction producing 42
   metal reacting with 53, 80, 81
   from plants and photosynthesis 20–1, 24, 28, 29
   and respiration 12, 24

pair, antagonistic 19, **124**
palisade layer 22
parachutes 110–11
particles 116
   'particle picture' 50
pascals 112, **127**
pelvis 18
pesticides 36, 43, **127**
pests 36–7, **127**
pH 48–9
   of soil 62–3
   of water 66
phosphates, in fertilisers 32
phosphorus, for plants 27, 33
photosynthesis 20–9, 30, 66, **127**
   and leaves 22–5
   and roots 26–7
physical weathering 65, **127**
pistons 114–15, **127**
pivot **127**
   and counterweights 120
   and levers 118, 119
   and moments 122, 123
planets *see* space and solar system
plants
   cells 8–9, 26
   dead, remains of 62
   fertilisation 8–9
   flowers 8–9, 27, 33
   growth of 20–1, 27, 34–7
   importance in environment 28–9
   reproduction 10
   selective breeding 8–9, **127**
   soil and 62–3
   see also leaves; photosynthesis; roots; trees
plants for food 25, 30–9, 76
   competition and growth 34–5, **125**
   and environment 28–9
   pests and growth 36–7, **127**
   soil pH and 63
   see also farming; fertilisers

plastics 76
pneumatics 116–17, **127**
polar, satellite 101, **127**
pollen 8–9
pollutants/pollution 66–7, **127**
   global warming 71, **126**
   monitoring 70, **126**
   from power stations 91
   reducing 69
   wasted electricity and 89
   see also acid rain
potassium 40
   in fertilisers 32
   for plants 27, 33
   reactivity 54, 55, 57
potassium chloride 49
potassium hydroxide 48, 49, 54
potato 63
   starch in 24, 31
power stations 69, 75, 90–1, 92, 117
pregnancy, and smoking 15
preservative, copper sulphate as 47
pressure 112–22, **127**
   atmospheric 117, **124**
   counterbalance 120–1, **125**
   hydraulics 114–16, **126**
   levers 118–19, **126**
   moments 122–3, **126**
   pneumatics 116–17, **127**
producers 30, **127**
   see also plants
protein
   in diet 13
   in plants 25, 27, 30, 33, 76
pterodactyl 120
pulling force *see* gravity
pushing 106–7
pyramid of numbers 37

radiation 89
rain, acid 64, 66–9, **124**
rainforests 29
rare breeds, conservation of 7
reactivity 52–61
   series 53, 55, 57, 60, **127**
   usefulness of 60–1
reactivity of metals
   and acids 42–5, 50–1, 52, 56–7, 65
   and air 52–3
   displacement 58–9, 74, **125**
   and water 54–5, 57
reactivity series **127**
recreational drugs 16
redwood tree 20
reproduction *see* asexual reproduction; sexual reproduction

resistance
   air 106, **124**
   to cold 8
   to rotting 8
respiration 12, 28, **127**
   glucose in 24
ribs 14, 18
rockets 74
   thrust 97, **128**
rocks 44, 64–5
   see also weathering
roots
   phosphorus for 27, 33
   and photosynthesis 25, 26–7
   root hair cells 26
   water absorbed by 26
rotting, resistance to 8
rust 52

safety, and alkalis 48
salt **127**
   from reactions with acids 42–7, 49, 56, 65
sandstone 68
sandy soil 62
satellites **127**
   artificial *see* artificial satellites
   natural 96, 99, 100, 106, **126**
   orbit 101, **125**
seconds 102, **127**
seeds 25, 31
seesaws 120, 122
selective breeding 6–9, **127**
selective weedkiller 35, **127**
sexual reproduction 3, 10, **127**
   identical twins 4
sheep breeding 7
shoot 25
side effects of drugs 16–17
silver
   reactivity 55, 57, 60, 61
   uses 61
skeleton 18
skull 18, 119
slowing down 106–7, 110–11
sodium 40
   reactivity 55, 57
sodium carbonate 44
sodium hydroxide 48
soils 62–3
   water in 20, 26, 62
   see also roots
solar system 98–101
   asteroids 99, 106
   models 98–9
   weight on planets 96
   see also satellites
sound energy 88

space 106
  Space Shuttle 75, 109, 111
  temperature of spacecraft 109
  see also solar system
spanner 119
speed 102–11, **127**
  acceleration 104–5, 108–9, 110, **124**
  and forces 106–7
  measuring 102–3, 104, **126**
  parachutes 110–11
  slowing down 106–7, 110–11
sperm cells and reproduction 2, 3, 4
spine 18
sport see exercise and sport
sprain 18, **127**, **128**
spring, energy stored in 83
starch in plants 23, 24, 30–1
steam engines 117
steep slope 104
stigma 8
storage
  of electricity not possible 91
  of energy 83
  of food see plants as food
strain 18, **128**
strawberries 10
streamlined 108, **128**
style 8
submarine and whale compared 108
sulphate 43, 45, 46, 47, 50–1, 58
sulphur dioxide 66–7
sulphuric acid 43, 45, 46, 50–1
Sun
  gravity of 99
  see also light; solar system
synthetic fibre 43
syringes 114, 116

tar 15, **128**
tarnished 52, **128**
teeth 119
temperature
  cooling plants 26
  resistance to cold 8
  of spacecraft 109
  thermal conduction 40, 89
  and weathering 64, 65
  see also heat energy
theory of conservation of mass 78–81, **128**
thermal conduction 40, 89
thigh 18
thrust 97, **128**
time **128**
  measurement 105
  and speed 102–3
tomatoes 5
trace elements 33, **128**
trachea (windpipe) 14, 15
transfer of energy 82, 84–5, 89, **128**
transformed energy 82, 84, 93, **128**
trees
  and acid rain 68
  carbon dioxide absorbed by 29
  oxygen emitted by 29
  photosynthesis 20
triceps 18, 119
turbine 90, **128**
turning moment 122

unbalanced forces 107, **128**
universal indicator 54
using chemistry 72–81
  conservation of mass 78–81, **128**
  new materials 76–7
  see also chemical reactions; electricity; fuels
uterus 4

variation
  environmental 5–6, **125**
  inherited 2–3, **126**
vegetables 8, 63
  starch in 24, 31
veins in leaf 22, 27
vitamins in diet 13
voltage 85, 86, 87, 88, **128**

warmth
  from food 12–13
  and plants 38
washing powder 49
wasted energy 92–3
water
  from combustion 72
  in diet 13
hydroelectric energy 91
and plants
  absorbed by roots 26
  for photosynthesis 20–1, 24, 26, 38–9
  loss prevented 23
  stolen by weeds 34
  travel 26–7
in power stations 90
from reactions with acids 44–5, 46, 49, 65
reactivity of metals with 54–5, 57
and respiration 12
in soils 20, 26, 62
and weathering 64, 65
see also dissolving; rain
wave energy 91
weather satellite 101
weathering 64–5, **128**
  chemical 64–5, **124**
  physical 65, **127**
weedkiller 35, **128**
  development of 77
  selective 35, **127**
weeds 34–5, **128**
weight **128**
  and gravity 94, 95, 96
  lifting 83
  measured in newtons 94, 95, **126**
  and speed 105, 110
whale, shape of 108
wind
  energy 82, 91
  weathering by 65
winter, survival of plants in 31
wood 25, 29, 74
word equations 21, 24, 50

xylem tubes in leaf 22, 26

zinc
  in electric cell 84
  reaction with acid 42, 50–1
  reactivity 56, 57, 58, 60
zinc sulphate 43, 50–1, 58